Secrets

of the

Selection
Committee

Create Proposals and Presentations that Win

GARY R. COOVER

Rollston Press

Secrets of the Selection Committee

by Gary R. Coover

ISBN-13: 978-0-9970748-0-2

ISBN-10: 0-9970748-0-9

ROLLSTON PRESS
330 N. Rollston Avenue
Fayetteville, AR 72701
USA

TABLE OF CONTENTS

PREFACE

Although the topics in this book could apply to selections based on price, it is primarily written for the selection of professional services and is written from the Selection Committee's point of view.

We're the ones on the receiving end of your carefully crafted works of art, or in many cases, your sloppily cobbled together wastes of paper, slides, time and effort.

The secrets in this book shouldn't be secrets at all, and most are not terribly earth-shattering. But they're secrets in the sense that most people have never been on a Selection Committee, or known anyone who was, or made more than a perfunctory effort to find out how the process works or why they should care.

This book will show you how to maximize your chances, not by heaping more stuff on the Selection Committee, but through a better understanding of exactly what we're looking for and how you can make it easier for us to pick you as the winner.

All of the stories and examples in the book are true – the names have been omitted to protect the guilty. With luck, these will be their stories and not yours. Let their mistakes be your caveats as you see your submittals anew through the eyes of the reviewers.

Your quals are only part of the equation. Other "secret" forces are often at work. Master these and you will win the eternal trust of the Selection Committee. Plus, win more projects!

Gary R. Coover
Honolulu, HI

INTRODUCTION

Somewhere in a closed room a large group of people are facing a huge pile of bound documents – Statements of Qualifications for upcoming projects or perhaps specific submittals responding to a Request for Proposal.

A short time is allotted to sort through potentially dozens of submittals containing hundreds of pages. Only one will be selected.

Or perhaps a chosen few will to go to the next round – The Shortlist Interview.

Your submittal is in that pile. Somewhere.

How will it fare?

Is it even worth reading?

Does it meet all the basic criteria?

How does it stack up against the competition?

Is it more awesome and selectable than everyone else's?

Your qualifications may be great, but they are just one piece of the puzzle. There are other considerations that will very likely influence and determine the final outcome.

They're not in writing.

Secrets, if you will.

If you know what they are and how to address them your submittals and presentations will have a significantly greater chance of being winners.

Welcome to the "secret" world of the Selection Committee.

This book will open the door.

WHO WE ARE

The Selection Committee holds the power of life and death over your submittal. So who exactly are these people and what goes on behind those closed doors?

Do you imagine cloaked judges, dart boards, tea leaves, Ouija Boards, perhaps even Magic 8-Balls?

It's not quite like that, but I'm sure there are times the entire committee would much rather resort to esoteric divination as opposed to slogging through an almost unsurmountable heap of paper filled with mind-numbing amounts of text and figures.

Think of it like this:

A selection committee is a one-time one-sided blind speed-date

...and you're not there, except in paper form only. That might be the only thing we have to know about you, and the only thing that will determine whether you make the cut or not.

You might be competing with a couple dozen other submittals, or maybe just a couple, there's no way for you to know.

But regardless of the height of the stack in front of us, our task is to find the best possible match between our immediate need and your abilities to address that need.

Unless we know you already, all we have to go by are the words, sentences, paragraphs, photographs and graphics you've chosen to show us.

We're not a mysterious secret society or a group of be-wigged and be-robed judges – we're just employees of the agency or company that's offering the solicitation to solve a particular problem.

With luck, most or all of us will be at least somewhat familiar with the project and its requirements.

There might be one of us, there might be a dozen of us. It depends on the size and complexity of the project.

It's seldom an easy process due to the sheer volume of submitted material and the rather short amount of time allocated for review and selection.

Keep in mind that we're only human, and instead of burying us in what Matt Handal (author of *Proposal Development Secrets*) calls "boilerplate drivel from your extensive library of crap," try writing and presenting something that will pique our interest and convince us as quickly as possible that you're "The One."

How you sell yourself and get your story across to us is of crucial importance – for both of us.

WHAT WE'RE LOOKING FOR

The perfect answer to The Big Question:

"Who is the best firm for our project?"

WHAT WE OFTEN GET

Heaping piles of slapped together gobbledegook that claims "we are leaders" in state-of-the-art expertise with extensive experience in everything but misses the key issues and the requirements of the RFP and has org charts that are difficult to read and decipher and résumés that were obviously just thrown in without any sense of what individual expertise we really need and projects that are just jumbled together with little relevance to the project experience we're looking for with endless paragraphs that just run on and on with high-sounding low performing pompous words and proprietary acronyms with everything written in passive tense and beaucoups of bold unsubstantiated claims about how wonderful they are and "we're the best" without giving any specific examples and crappy photographs that don't show much of anything along with godawful graphics and tired clip art that is just thrown in gratuitously and often in strange fonts and odd paragraph justifications and with a liberal sprinkling of missspellings and glaring typos and garbled writing and this is often accompanied with all sorts of odd sections and dividers with excess filler and fluff in the form of corporate brochures and company publications that are full of excessive bs and blah blah blah...

Aaaaaaaaargh!

Trust me, there's a much better way to do this.

THE WORLD OF ACRONYMIA

But before we go any further...

A most unfortunate and totally necessary part of all technical, governmental and military work is the use of acronyms and abbreviations to make complex names and phrases easier to understand. Once you know what they are, of course.

It's the wading through the alphabet soup that's the hard part.

Technically speaking, acronyms are abbreviations that can be pronounced like words. For example, MATOC is pronounced just like it looks while RFP is not. For this book we'll incorrectly call everything an acronym for the sake of abbreviation.

Acronym Rule #1

Know your client's acronyms.

If you can't understand or speak their language, then why do you think you would have any chance of ever working for them?

Acronym Rule #2

Don't make clients learn (or guess) yours.

You're not a secret society or an exclusive club. **We don't care about any of the internal acronyms peculiar to your company.** They have no meaning for us, so never use them outside your own firm.

Of course, the proposal world has its own collection of obscure acronyms. Here are the ones you are most likely to encounter in government work:

8(a)	Social & Economic Disadvantaged SBA Program
AIA	American Institute of Architects
CA	Construction Administration
CAGE	Commercial and Government Entity Code
CCM	Certified Construction Manager
CFR	Code of Federal Regulations
CIP	Capital Improvement Plan
COB	Close of Business
COR	Contracting Officer's Representative
COTR	Contracting Officer's Technical Representative
DB	Design-Build
DBB	Design-Bid-Build
DBE	Disadvantaged Business Enterprise
DBIA	Design-Build Institute of America
DOD	Department of Defense
DOR	Designer of Record
DSBS	Dynamic Small Business Search (SBA)
EIN	Employer Identification Number
EOD	End of Day
FAR	Federal Acquisition Regulations
FBO	Fed Biz Opps (www.fedbizopps.gov)

FFP	Firm Fixed Price
GSA	General Services Administration
HUBZone	Historically Underutilized Business Zone
IDC	Indefinite Delivery Contract
IDIQ	Indefinite Delivery Indefinite Quantity
KO	Contracting Officer
LEED	Leadership in Energy & Environmental Design
LPTA	Lowest Price Technically Acceptable
LS	Lump Sum
MACC	Multiple Award Construction Contract
MATOC	Multiple Award Task Order Contract
MBE	Minority Business Enterprise
MEP	Mechanical, Electrical, Plumbing
MEPF	Mechanical, Electrical, Plumbing, Fire Protection
MILCON	Military Construction
NAICS	North American Industry Classification System
NAVFAC	Naval Facilities Engineering Command
NTP	Notice to Proceed
PE	Professional Engineer
PLS	Professional Land Surveyor
PM	Project Manager
PO	Purchase Order
POC	Point of Contact

Secrets of the Selection Committee

PS&E	Plans, Specifications and Estimates
QAP	Quality Assurance Plan
QCP	Quality Control Plan
RFI	Request for Information
RFP	Request for Proposal
RFQ	Request for Qualifications
SAM	System for Award Management
SATOC	Single Award Task Order Contract
SB	Small Business
SBA	Small Business Administration
SDVOSB	Service-Disabled Veteran-Owned Small Business
Set-Aside	(only certain types of firms can submit)
SF330	US Government Standard Form 330
SOQ	Statement of Qualifications
Sources Sought	(a marketing inquiry for a future set-aside)
SOW	Statement of Work
T&M	Time & Materials
TBD	To Be Determined
USACE	United States Army Corps of Engineers
USGBC	US Green Building Council
VOSB	Veteran-Owned Small Business
WBE	Woman-owned Business Enterprise
WOSB	Woman-Owned Small Business

...plus about a gazillion others.

Make your own list of acronyms, keep it current, and make sure your marketing coordinators and proposal writers understand them all thoroughly and use them correctly.

Acronym Rule #3

Never ever use any cutesy acronyms from the world of texting or internet chat in any of your proposals, emails or correspondence with clients or prospective clients. Never.

BTW, IDK , BFF, AFIK, IMHO, LOL, ROTFLMAO, WTF

THE SELECTION PROCESS

Procurement, acquisition, selection – all names for the process of finding the best firm/vendor/contractor to perform specific functions to meet a client's/customer's particular needs.

There are many different types of selections for different types of projects, including:

Sole Source

Qualifications-Based

Best Value

Lowest Price

Sole Source is the best if you can get it – if you meet all the qualifications they can just hand the project to you. Sweet. This can also be the case if you have an approved GSA Schedule.

It doesn't happen very often, usually only for very small projects or products or if you happen to meet certain socio-economic criteria making you eligible for sole source set-asides.

Qualifications-Based Selection (QBS) is the most common for professional services. Certainly for architects and engineers in the governmental sector due to the Brooks Act passed in 1972 requiring the U.S. Federal Government to select engineering and architecture firms based upon their qualifications and experience instead of price.

Best Value allows the client to select the firm (or product) they feel gives the best value, regardless of price.

Lowest Price is exactly that. A commodity-level selection often giving clients little recourse other than to accept lowest price. This is most often the case in construction contracts and product procurements.

SOQ's vs RFP's

Professional services are most often procured one of two ways.

A **Statement of Qualifications (SOQ)** is a submittal that outlines a firm's general strengths and interests. These are typically submitted for consideration for unspecified upcoming projects, in many cases on an annual basis for government agencies and municipalities.

A **Request for Proposal (RFP)** is issued for a specific project and only submittals that respond to the RFP will be considered for selection.

Two paths

The selection procedure is essentially the same for both SOQ's and RFP's:

1. Initial submittal screening
2. Selection Committee meeting
3. Final Selection

If several firms are considered sufficiently qualified and no clear winner is chosen, the process becomes:

1. Initial submittal screening
2. Selection Committee meeting
3. Short List Selection
4. Interview Presentation
5. Final Selection

Secrets of the Selection Committee

The Selection Meeting

Once the members of a Selection Committee have themselves been selected, they will usually meet at a specific time and place to all go through the pile of proposals.

Sometimes proposals are rated individually by each reviewer using a scorecard with the results collected and tabulated at the end of the session.

In other instances it can be much less formal, with a winner selected by acclamation after general discussion. It depends on the client/agency, and how defensible the selection might need to be in case of a protest.

With more and more submittals being electronic these days there might not even be an official meeting. It might all happen separately and independently with files passed or posted electronically. Some submittals could even be subjected to automated screening software.

Four key factors that impact your selection

1. Your Qualifications

2. Your Relationship/Reputation

3. Your Submittal/Interview

4. Outside Forces

The Review Process

0. Initial completeness check by staff

1. Quick scan of cover to see who from, does the name ring any bells or jog the memory?

2. Quick scan of the Cover Letter to check for principal commitment (or ignore altogether)

3. Read Executive Summary. Short, sweet and to the point? Or rambling mish-mash?

4. Study Org Chart – who's who, all bases covered, good subconsultant team members?

5. Quick Résumé Check – who do we know, is this the A-Team, skills & experience?

6. Scan Projects – similar size & complexity, relevant, location, similar type of client?

7. Project Understanding/Approach – canned or customized?

8. Answer all questions in the RFP?

9. Proof the team has played well together previously?

10. References ok?

11. Any issues, good or bad?

12. Shortlist pile or toss

13. Deeper review if warranted

14. Cuss & Discuss

15. Overall opinion or scorecard

16. Select (Shortlist or Final)

EVALUATION CRITERIA

Eeny meeny miny moe...

Not exactly.

But we do need a way of determining who is best suited to the task, so we resort to various methodical ways and means of evaluating your submittal, your interview presentation, your past performance and your potential for future success.

There are two types of evaluations,

1. After your previous project is finished.

2. When you are being considered for the next project.

If you're familiar with both then you will be better equipped to answer our questions and address our concerns.

The following pages present evaluation criteria used by a wide variety of government agencies. Know and understand why they are asking these specific questions.

Even though these criteria may not appear in a particular RFP you can be assured that they are looking for all of these specific things.

If you can, address all of these issues in your submittal whether asked for or not.

These are the things clients are looking for. Give it to them.

US Army Corps of Engineers

Evaluation Steps:

1. Conduct Preproposal Training.

2. Perform Initial Screening of Proposals.

3. Identify and Document Areas of the Proposal that are resolvable through clarifications or communications.

4. Prepare an Initial Evaluation Identifying and Documenting Proposal Deficiencies, Strengths, Weaknesses, Risks and Associated Items for Negotiation.

5. Assign Ratings for Non-Cost Evaluation Factors when using the Tradeoff Process.

6. Prepare a Summary Evaluation Report.

WORLD BANK

Scorecard Criteria

- Experience
- Methodology
- Proposed Staff
- Training
- Local Input
- Individual Qualifications
- Adequacy for the Assignment
- Experience in Region

ASIAN DEVELOPMENT BANK

- Firm's Qualifications and Experience
- Approach & Methodology
- Proposed Biodata
- Work Plan

US Army Corps of Engineers

Architect-Engineer Contracting in USACE
Pamphlet EP 715-1-7, 2012

Primary Selection Criteria (in order of importance)

    A.   Specialized Experience and Technical Competence

    B.   Professional Qualifications

    C.   Past Performance

    D.   Capacity

    E.   Knowledge of the Locality

Secondary Selection Criteria (to be used as a tie-breaker)

    A.   SB and SDB Participation

    B.   Geographic Proximity

    C.   Volume of DoD Contract Awards

"General experience working for certain customers, such as DoD, Army, Air Force, or USACE, is not an appropriate selection criterion. Instead, the selection criteria should address experience in certain types of projects or work, and knowledge of essential laws, regulations and/or criteria."

"A firm may not be eliminated simply for failing to submit certain information or for altering the format of a SF 330. However, a firm may be recommended as not qualified or ranked low if missing, confusing, conflicting, obsolete or obscure information prevents a board from reasonably determining that a firm demonstrates certain required qualifications."

           Secrets of the Selection Committee

Department of Defense

Form DD 2631

17. DESIGN PHASE OR ENGINEERING SERVICES *(Quality of A-E Services Evaluation)*

ATTRIBUTES *(If applicable)*	EXCEP-TIONAL	VERY GOOD	SATIS-FACTORY	MARGINAL	UNSATIS-FACTORY
Thoroughness of Site Investigation/Field Analysis					
Quality Control Procedures and Execution					
Plans/Specs Accurate and Coordinated					
Plans Clear and Detailed Sufficiently					
Management and Adherence to Schedules					
Meeting Cost Limitations					
Suitability of Design or Study Results					
Solution Environmentally Suitable					
Cooperativeness and Responsiveness					
Quality of Briefing and Presentations					
Innovative Approaches/Technologies					
Implementation of Sm. Business Subcontracting Plan					

18. HOW MANY 100% FINAL RESUBMITTALS WERE REQUIRED BECAUSE OF POOR A-E PERFORMANCE?

19. CONSTRUCTION PHASE *(Quality of A-E Services Evaluation)*

ATTRIBUTES *(If applicable)*	EXCEP-TIONAL	VERY GOOD	SATIS-FACTORY	MARGINAL	UNSATIS-FACTORY
Plans Clear and Detailed Sufficiently					
Drawings Reflect True Conditions					
Plans/Specs Accurate and Coordinated					
Design Constructibility					
Cooperativeness and Responsiveness					
Timeliness and Quality of Processing Submittals					
Product & Equipment Selections Readily Available					
Timeliness of Answers to Design Questions					
Field Consultation and Investigations					
Quality of Construction Support Services					

City of Austin, Texas

- Timeliness of Performance

- Budget/Cost Control

- Quality of Work Performed

- Invoicing and Payments

- Compliance with Minority and Women Owned Business Program

- Deliverables

- Regulatory Compliance and Permitting

Nebraska Department of Roads (NDOR)

- Communication & Cooperation

- Quality

- Recordkeeping

- Timeliness of Deliverables and Responses to Owner Requests

- Scope & Budget

- Project Manager

- Technical Performance

City of Williamsburg, VA

- Similar Projects
- Leadership Structure
- Management Approach
- Financial Condition
- Reputation/Experience of Team

Florida Department of Transportation

(FDOT)

- Administration of Contract
- Management of Issues and Resources
- Communication, Documentation and Coordination
- Execution of Work (schedule, budget, quality control, scope)
- Post-Design Activities

Naval Facilities Engineering Command

(NAVFAC)

How to be selected:

- Professional qualifications necessary for satisfactory performance of required services.

- Specialized experience and technical competence in the type of work required.

- Capacity to accomplish the work in the required time.

- Experience in sustainable design.

- Established quality control program.

- Past performance on contracts with Government agencies and private industry in terms of cost control, quality of work, subcontracting and compliance with performance schedules.

- Location in the general geographical area of the project and knowledge of the locality of the project, provided that application of this criterion leaves an appropriate number of qualified firms, given the nature and size of the project.

- Demonstrated success in prescribing the use of recovered materials and achieving waste reduction and energy efficiency in utility design.

- Acceptability under other appropriate evaluation criteria.

NAVFAC/USACE Past Performance Questionnaire

Form PPQ-0

NAVFAC/USACE PAST PERFORMANCE QUESTIONNAIRE (Form PPQ-0)
CONTRACT INFORMATION (Contractor to complete Blocks 1-4)
1. Contractor Information Firm Name: CAGE Code: Address: DUNs Number: Phone Number: Email Address: Point of Contact: Contact Phone Number:
2. Work Performed as: ☐ Prime Contractor   ☐ Sub Contractor   ☐ Joint Venture   ☐ Other (Explain) Percent of project work performed: If subcontractor, who was the prime (Name/Phone #):
3. Contract Information Contract Number: Delivery/Task Order Number (if applicable): Contract Type: ☐ Firm Fixed Price   ☐ Cost Reimbursement   ☐ Other (Please specify): Contract Title: Contract Location: Award Date (mm/dd/yy): Contract Completion Date (mm/dd/yy): Actual Completion Date (mm/dd/yy): Explain Differences: Original Contract Price (Award Amount): Final Contract Price (*to include all modifications, if applicable*): Explain Differences:
4. Project Description: Complexity of Work ☐ High   ☐ Med   ☐ Routine How is this project relevant to project of submission? (*Please provide details such as similar equipment, requirements, conditions, etc.*)
CLIENT INFORMATION (Client to complete Blocks 5-8)
5. Client Information Name: Title: Phone Number: Email Address:
6. Describe the client's role in the project:
7. Date Questionnaire was completed (mm/dd/yy):
8. Client's Signature:

NOTE: NAVFAC REQUESTS THAT THE CLIENT COMPLETES THIS QUESTIONNAIRE AND SUBMITS DIRECTLY BACK TO THE OFFEROR. THE OFFEROR WILL SUBMIT THE COMPLETED QUESTIONNAIRE TO NAVFAC WITH THEIR PROPOSAL, AND MAY DUPLICATE THIS QUESTIONNAIRE FOR FUTURE SUBMISSION ON NAVFAC SOLICITATIONS. CLIENTS ARE HIGHLY ENCOURAGED TO SUBMIT QUESTIONNAIRES DIRECTLY TO THE OFFEROR. HOWEVER, QUESTIONNAIRES MAY BE SUBMITTED DIRECTLY TO NAVFAC. PLEASE CONTACT THE OFFEROR FOR NAVFAC POC INFORMATION. THE GOVERNMENT RESERVES THE RIGHT TO VERIFY ANY AND ALL INFORMATION ON THIS FORM.

Contractor Information (Firm Name): _____

Client Information (Name): _____

PLEASE CIRCLE THE ADJECTIVE RATING WHICH BEST REFLECTS
YOUR EVALUATION OF THE CONTRACTOR'S PERFORMANCE.

1. QUALITY:						
a) Quality of technical data/report preparation efforts	E	VG	S	M	U	N
b) Ability to meet quality standards specified for technical performance	E	VG	S	M	U	N
c) Timeliness/effectiveness of contract problem resolution without extensive customer guidance	E	VG	S	M	U	N
d) Adequacy/effectiveness of quality control program and adherence to contract quality assurance requirements (without adverse effect on performance)	E	VG	S	M	U	N
2. SCHEDULE/TIMELINESS OF PERFORMANCE:						
a) Compliance with contract delivery/completion schedules including any significant intermediate milestones. *(If liquidated damages were assessed or the schedule was not met, please address below)*	E	VG	S	M	U	N
b) Rate the contractor's use of available resources to accomplish tasks identified in the contract	E	VG	S	M	U	N
3. CUSTOMER SATISFACTION:						
a) To what extent were the end users satisfied with the project?	E	VG	S	M	U	N
b) Contractor was reasonable and cooperative in dealing with your staff (including the ability to successfully resolve disagreements/disputes; responsiveness to administrative reports, businesslike and communication)	E	VG	S	M	U	N
c) To what extent was the contractor cooperative, businesslike, and concerned with the interests of the customer?	E	VG	S	M	U	N
d) Overall customer satisfaction	E	VG	S	M	U	N
4. MANAGEMENT/ PERSONNEL/LABOR						
a) Effectiveness of on-site management, including management of subcontractors, suppliers, materials, and/or labor force?	E	VG	S	M	U	N
b) Ability to hire, apply, and retain a qualified workforce to this effort	E	VG	S	M	U	N
c) Government Property Control	E	VG	S	M	U	N
d) Knowledge/expertise demonstrated by contractor personnel	E	VG	S	M	U	N
e) Utilization of Small Business concerns	E	VG	S	M	U	N
f) Ability to simultaneously manage multiple projects with multiple disciplines	E	VG	S	M	U	N
g) Ability to assimilate and incorporate changes in requirements and/or priority, including planning, execution and response to Government changes	E	VG	S	M	U	N
h) Effectiveness of overall management (including ability to effectively lead, manage and control the program)	E	VG	S	M	U	N
5. COST/FINANCIAL MANAGEMENT						
a) Ability to meet the terms and conditions within the contractually agreed price(s)?	E	VG	S	M	U	N

Contractor Information (Firm Name): _____

Client Information (Name): _____

b) Contractor proposed innovative alternative methods/processes that reduced cost, improved maintainability or other factors that benefited the client	E	VG	S	M	U	N
c) If this is/was a Government cost type contract, please rate the Contractor's timeliness and accuracy in submitting monthly invoices with appropriate back-up documentation, monthly status reports/budget variance reports, compliance with established budgets and avoidance of significant and/or unexplained variances (under runs or overruns)	E	VG	S	M	U	N
d) Is the Contractor's accounting system adequate for management and tracking of costs? *If no, please explain in Remarks section.*		Yes			No	
e) If this is/was a Government contract, has/was this contract been partially or completely terminated for default or convenience or are there any pending terminations? *Indicate if show cause or cure notices were issued, or any default action in comment section below.*		Yes			No	
f) Have there been any indications that the contractor has had any financial problems? *If yes, please explain below.*		Yes			No	
6. SAFETY/SECURITY						
a) To what extent was the contractor able to maintain an environment of safety, adhere to its approved safety plan, and respond to safety issues? (Includes: following the users rules, regulations, and requirements regarding housekeeping, safety, correction of noted deficiencies, etc.)	E	VG	S	M	U	N
b) Contractor complied with all security requirements for the project and personnel security requirements.	E	VG	S	M	U	N
7. GENERAL						
a) Ability to successfully respond to emergency and/or surge situations (including notifying COR, PM or Contracting Officer in a timely manner regarding urgent contractual issues).	E	VG	S	M	U	N
b) Compliance with contractual terms/provisions *(explain if specific issues)*	E	VG	S	M	U	N
c) Would you hire or work with this firm again? *(If no, please explain below)*		Yes			No	
d) In summary, provide an overall rating for the work performed by this contractor.	E	VG	S	M	U	N

Please provide responses to the questions above (*if applicable*) and/or additional remarks. Furthermore, please provide a brief narrative addressing specific strengths, weaknesses, deficiencies, or other comments which may assist our office in evaluating performance risk *(please attach additional pages if necessary)***:**

RATING	DEFINITION	NOTE
(E) Exceptional	Performance meets contractual requirements and exceeds many to the Government/Owner's benefit. The contractual performance of the element or sub-element being assessed was accomplished with few minor problems for which corrective actions taken by the contractor was highly effective.	An Exceptional rating is appropriate when the Contractor successfully performed multiple significant events that were of benefit to the Government/Owner. A singular benefit, however, could be of such magnitude that it alone constitutes an Exceptional rating. Also, there should have been NO significant weaknesses identified.
(VG) Very Good	Performance meets contractual requirements and exceeds some to the Government's/Owner's benefit. The contractual performance of the element or sub-element being assessed was accomplished with some minor problems for which corrective actions taken by the contractor were effective.	A Very Good rating is appropriate when the Contractor successfully performed a significant event that was a benefit to the Government/Owner. There should have been no significant weaknesses identified.
(S) Satisfactory	Performance meets minimum contractual requirements. The contractual performance of the element or sub-element contains some minor problems for which corrective actions taken by the contractor appear or were satisfactory.	A Satisfactory rating is appropriate when there were only minor problems, or major problems that the contractor recovered from without impact to the contract. There should have been NO significant weaknesses identified. Per DOD policy, a fundamental principle of assigning ratings is that contractors will not be assessed a rating lower than Satisfactory solely for not performing beyond the requirements of the contract.
(M) Marginal	Performance does not meet some contractual requirements. The contractual performance of the element or sub-element being assessed reflects a serious problem for which the contractor has not yet identified corrective actions. The contractor's proposed actions appear only marginally effective or were not fully implemented.	A Marginal is appropriate when a significant event occurred that the contractor had trouble overcoming which impacted the Government/Owner.
(U) Unsatisfactory	Performance does not meet most contractual requirements and recovery is not likely in a timely manner. The contractual performance of the element or sub-element contains serious problem(s) for which the contractor's corrective actions appear or were ineffective.	An Unsatisfactory rating is appropriate when multiple significant events occurred that the contractor had trouble overcoming and which impacted the Government/Owner. A singular problem, however, could be of such serious magnitude that it alone constitutes an unsatisfactory rating.
(N) Not Applicable	No information or did not apply to your contract	Rating will be neither positive nor negative.

ARMY SOURCE SELECTION MANUAL

Definitions of Key Evaluation Terms

Rating – The evaluators' conclusions (supported by narrative writeups) identifying the strengths, weaknesses, and deficiencies of an evaluation factor or subfactor. The ratings for the Technical Factor and each of its Subfactors will be expressed as an adjective.

Deficiency – A material failure of a proposal to meet a Government requirement or a combination of significant weaknesses in a proposal that increases the risk of unsuccessful contract performance to an unacceptable level.

Strength – Any aspect of a proposal that, when judged against a stated evaluation criterion, enhances the merit of the proposal or increases the probability of successful performance of the contract.

Significant Strength – A significant strength appreciably enhances the merit of a proposal or appreciably increases the probability of successful contract performance.

Weakness – A flaw in a proposal that increases the risk of unsuccessful contract performance.

Significant Weakness – A flaw that appreciably increases the risk of unsuccessful contract performance.

ARMY SOURCE SELECTION MANUAL

RATING: EXCELLENT

The proposal has exceptional merit and reflects an excellent approach which will clearly result in the superior attainment of all requirements and objectives.

This clearly achievable approach includes numerous advantageous characteristics of substance, and essentially no disadvantages, which can be expected to result in outstanding performance.

The risk of unsuccessful performance is very low as the proposal provides solutions which are unquestionably feasible and practical.

These solutions are further considered very low risk in that they are exceptionally clear and precise, fully supported, and demonstrate a clear understanding of the requirements.

Risk Level: Very Low

Essentially <u>no doubt</u> exists that the offeror will successfully perform the required effort based on their performance record.

ARMY SOURCE SELECTION MANUAL

RATING: UNACCEPTABLE

The proposal demonstrates an approach which, based on a very high risk, will very likely not be capable of meeting all requirements and objectives.

This approach has numerous disadvantages of substance, and advantages which, if they exist, are far outweighed by disadvantages.

Collectively, the advantages and disadvantages will not result in satisfactory performance.

The risk of unsuccessful performance is very high as the proposal contains solutions which are not feasible and practical.

The solutions are further considered to reflect very high risk in that they lack any clarity or precision, are unsupported, and do not demonstrate an understanding of the requirement.

Risk Level: Very High

It is **extremely doubtful** that the offeror will successfully perform the required effort based on their performance record.

USACE Past Performance Risk Assessment Questionnaire

A. Compliance of Products, Services, Documents, and Related Deliverables to Specification Requirements and Standards of Good Workmanship.

B. Effectiveness of Project Management (to include use and control of subcontractors).

C. Timeliness of Performance for Services and Product Deliverables, including the Administrative Aspects of Performance.

D. Effectiveness in Forecasting and Controlling Project Cost.

E. Commitment to Customer Satisfaction and Business-like Concern for its Customers' Interest.

F. Overall Satisfaction.

G. General Comments.

Oregon Department of Transportation (ODOT)

Consultant Evaluation Form

Cost/Budget

- Made good faith effort to collaboratively resolve negotiation issues.
- Finished within budget, including all amendments.
- Identified and implemented cost savings/efficiencies (including travel and ODCs) or ways to reduce per-unit costs.
- Limited the number of Contractor-initiated amendments.

Technical Quality

- Met work product standards; where practical, with minimal review.
- Responded to Agency comments in subsequent submission.
- Identified and implemented value added design services.
- Performed and documented QA/QC in a clear, concise manner.

Communications

- Produced clear, concise oral and written communication.
- Responded promptly to Agency and LPA comments/ requests.
- Notified Agency early regarding schedule issues.
- ODOT Stakeholders, the Public, local stakeholders, governmental agencies, local elected officials were kept informed of project scope, schedule, budget, and community impact.

Management

- Submitted accurate and timely progress reports, schedules and invoices.
- Conducted meetings efficiently.
- Responsive; coordinated with Agency effectively and collaboratively, adapted to changes requested by Agency.

Schedule

- Met milestones or due dates to meet bid let date and complete project within schedule including amendments (with minimal prompting from Agency).

Colorado Department of Transportation (CDOT)

Consultant Selection Factors and Considerations

STATEMENT OF INTEREST

Firm (Prime) Capability

- Firm's size, organization structure and flexibility.
- Production facilities and key capabilities such as CADD, etc.
- Firm's technical disciplines and the capabilities of subconsultants included on the team.

Past Experience of Similar Projects with Similar Teams

- Demonstrated ability to control costs.
- Demonstrated ability to do quality work.
- Demonstrated ability to meet schedule.

Project Team / Capacity

- Qualifications and ability of professional personnel (show years of experience and similar project experience).
- Experience and similar projects as a team.
- Commitment of key members.

Work Location

- Team's work location relative to the project location.
- Accessibility of the project team for coordination with the CDOT Project Manager and project location.

WORK PLAN

Project Goals

- Firm demonstrated understanding of the project goals.
- A list of deliverables required on the project.
- For non-project specific contracts, use a hypothetical project.

Project Control

- Cost Control:
    1. Controlling the consultant contract costs.
    2. Controlling the construction costs (if relevant) to stay within budget.
- Quality Control:
    1. Insuring that CDOT procedures are followed where appropriate.
    2. Insuring that project plans, specs and estimates are free of errors and meet CDOT and other agency standards.
- Schedule:
    1. Managing the required work to meet established schedule.
    2. A detailed work hour schedule should NOT be included.

Project Concept

- Has the firm formulated a successful approach to the project?
- Where appropriate, are possible design alternatives suggested?
- Where appropriate, have you exhibited a sensitivity to the general public concerns?
- Has the firm demonstrated a clear and concise understanding of the project based on the data which has been provided?

Project Critical Issues

- Are the major problems identified?
- Are the discussed problems significant?
- Are possible solutions reasonable?

YOUR QUALIFICATIONS

Now that you know what we're looking for, how well do you measure up?

This next part is totally up to you.

It's the sum total of your abilities and work experience.

But,

it's not everything you've ever done –

only what is pertinent to the specific RFP.

If your qualifications are a perfect match for the RFP, then you're well on your way to a potential win.

If you're nowhere close, and if there are no extenuating circumstances that would guarantee a good chance for a win, then you need to have the wherewithal to pass and not waste everyone's time.

But in between these two extremes is where the challenge is, how best to showcase what you know and what you can do.

Every project typically requires a multitude of skills, many of which are applicable regardless of specific project type. These are the ones you want to especially emphasize.

Sure it's important to know the ins and outs of the technical side of things, but it's how you use your knowledge and your tools to create successful outcomes that matters most.

Qualifications is not just about technical prowess, it's about the whole package you bring to the table.

Your experience & abilities

What have you done, what can you do, and what do you do well?

Experience is what you've done – expertise is what you're good at. With luck, you don't have one without the other.

Know what you're capable of and don't overreach unnecessarily or try to fake it. If you find you're missing a discipline or skill, then supplement your strengths with strong subconsultants.

But also realize that your experience and abilities are not always limited to just one project description.

For example, a street design project can be much more than a street design project – it can also include more universally applicable things such as planning, permitting, conceptual plans, cost estimates, charrettes, utility coordination, infrastructure relocation, easements, right-of-way determinations, public meetings, project management, calculations, conflict resolution, value engineering, QA/QC, construction observation, etc. that are tasks and skills that can be applied to many other types of future projects.

The subject matter is important, but we also want to know how you handle your projects, large or small, regardless of subject matter.

Have your projects typically been on-time, on-budget, and successful for your clients?

Have you a developed a particular expertise that's worth crowing about? Have you amassed an impressive catalog of lessons learned?

What are you best at and what are you known for?

Take a hard look at the skills used on your projects – you might have amassed a lot more experience than you think.

Your staff

If you are a design firm, your people are your most important and only asset. Without them you're just a collection of used office furniture.

So finding ways to showcase your current staff and their amazing abilities is key to winning projects.

It doesn't matter one bit if your company has a wonderful past history if no one on the current staff worked on those projects.

If you once had rock star employees or amazingly talented founders, they'd better still be around if you plan on trading on their laurels.

Clients are finally getting smarter these days about the huge difference between corporate experience and staff experience.

So it's who you have now that's important to you, and to us.

We want to know all about them, what they're good at, what makes them tick, why they do the things they do, how they think, and how they'll rise to the occasion to overcome any obstacles that might arise in our project.

We also want you to show us a wide variety of skills and abilities – we don't want all chiefs or all Indians, or all young or all old.

Give us a strong well-balanced team with complementary skills and strengths.

Give us a team of winners.

But maybe it was really really good coffee...

Don't just list the details of the projects your people worked on, tell us their role and what they actually did on those projects. Why were they important for the project's success?

Were they the chief cook?

Or just the bottle washer?

Generated calculations and reports?

Or just reviewed them?

Made crucial decisions in the field?

Or sat at a desk and pushed paper?

I once saw a SF330 résumé where all five of the project descriptions stated "Mr. XYZ assisted with..."

So you tell me, what did he actually do? If you're the reviewer, what does this tell you about his capabilities?

Perhaps he only made the coffee every morning?!?

Your projects

For a variety of very good reasons most RFP's ask you to only include projects you've worked on in the past 5 years.

Why? Staff turnover, market changes, technological advancements – lots of things can make your old projects... *really old.*

And of little real relevance to today's RFP.

You should include your most recent projects of similar scope, size and complexity. And instead of giving us long-winded rehashes of the statement of work or a laundry list of excessive data, focus on the key issues that we might care about and then tell us your specific responsibilities and actions.

Maybe even include some lessons learned or how you turned constraints into opportunities. Turned lemons into lemonade? We want to hear it!

Tell us the story, don't do a data dump.

And don't just give us a bunch of text either.

Give us context, give us meaning.

Include some high quality photos that tell us loads of information visually.

Many firms include special text boxes on their project sheets to highlight specific project tasks or results. We like that.

Rethink how you present your project data so it tells how you and the project and the client were successful. If you just give us lists or mountains of data we'll have no proof if any were on-time or on-budget. Or if the clients or end-users were happy with you or not.

Not so boring after all?

What if there's nothing extraordinary about your projects?

Maybe that's a good thing. So capitalize on it.

Instead of too many nitty gritty details, focus on what made them successful.

Maybe something like this:

Deadlines Missed = 0

City Review Submittals = 1

RFI's = 0

Budget Overruns =0

Happy Contractor = TRUE

Happy Client = TRUE

Happy End Users = TRUE

Project Praise = "Best plans we've ever seen"
             (XYZ Construction)

See, it almost doesn't matter what the project was about.

Your reputation

A powerful combination of qualifications and renown, your reputation is without a doubt the most valuable thing you own.

Like a fine wine or an aged scotch whisky it's shaped over time and is totally defined by the results you've been able to achieve from your efforts up to this point.

Believe it or not, there are many professional service and product delivery firms who need to do no additional marketing or promotion whatsoever other than just conduct their business as usual.

For most governmental projects they will still need to submit a Statement of Qualifications and respond to specific RFP's, but these pieces of paper only serve to throw their hat into the ring and are little more than confirmations of their known abilities.

Conversely, you may have all the experience in the world but if you're known for shoddy work or being late or being difficult these liabilities can easily tarnish your reputation and give your firm a black eye that could be well-nigh impossible to recover from.

Everything you do, everything you write, and everything you say is a reflection of your company's character and it can mean all the difference in the world when you are up in front of a Selection Committee.

The reluctant record holder

It's always good to be known for something, and to be number one, right?

Well, one engineering firm I worked for had the dubious distinction of having received the most plan review comments *ever* from the local water utility agency.

Not a handful, not a page, but 192 total comments and corrections. For one simple subdivision plan submittal.

192!!!

What do you think their chances were for ever doing any work for this government agency?

Zero. Or less.

And what do you suppose they told their colleagues at the other government agencies?

Once the word gets out about something like this there's no taking it back. It's almost impossible to correct without heads rolling, major sucking up, and damn near perfect plans forever after.

Differentiation

The best way to show how you are unique and uniquely qualified is to provide definitive examples that will resonate with the client and members of the Selection Committee.

If you really do stand out from the crowd, then you need to demonstrate why that is so. We need proof.

If you have developed any unique programs or procedures that drastically improve your quality and efficiency, then it's vitally important that you explain why they're so great.

What makes you different from everybody else?

What makes you special?

What makes you the best company for the RFP?

Maybe think about creating some simple little inserts like this:

Armchair Engineering

Good enough for them. Not for us.

Every site is unique. Surveys only tell part of the story. How can anyone design site improvements without personally seeing it and walking the walk?

We visit every site at early on, usually before the proposal is even started. Gotta see it to know it. Oh sure, we take lots of pictures, but it's what our engineers see for themselves that really counts. And it's what sets us apart from the others who never leave their desks.

Don't be invisible

You might think it's all well and good to sit in your office all day cranking out beautiful architectural or engineering plans, but if no one else knows about it then you stand a very good chance of being a complete unknown in front of a Selection Committee. And that's not good.

People hire folks they know and trust, simple as that. If we don't know you, then there's a good chance you'll be passed over.

But there are much better ways of getting the word out as opposed to blindly responding to every RFP in hopes that you'll eventually be recognized and win. It's not a numbers game.

You may not realize it, but members of Selection Committees are often members of your professional community as well as being members your local community. If you and your company are out and about doing great things in the community you stand a very good chance of making a good impression before you've ever responded to an RFP.

Are you a member of your local professional societies? Do you have a positive presence at public meetings, perhaps as a board member or planning commission member? Do you participate in community activities and charity events?

How about presenting or emceeing at local, regional and state professional conferences? Have you written any white papers or interesting blogs? Do you use social media to enhance your brand and your professional status?

Try to get to know potential Selection Committee members face to face. Not to sell them or influence them, but just to make sure they know who you are.

"Out of sight, out of mind" can be frighteningly true.

The Kiss of Death: "Oh, are they still around?"

Spread the news

How many of you have a corporate newsletter that you send to clients and potential Selection Committee members? How many of them totally suck? I thought so.

We don't care about your staff birthdays or babies or lame jokes or stupid clip art. That's maybe ok for an internal newsletter but that's not how you impress your clients.

"But we don't have the time or the staff to write a newsletter."

Guess what, you don't need time or staff – it's a lot easier than you think. I used to write them in under 30 minutes from start to finish including hitting "send." Once a month, on my lunch hour. So, no excuses.

The trick is to keep 'em short, informative and entertaining, and make it something that can be read quickly in 5 minutes or less.

Make it the body of the email itself. Standard fonts, no graphics and no attachments. Many governmental and military email servers can't accept attachments anyway. Just write two or three paragraphs about you and your projects. Make it folksy and fun to read, nothing too technical.

Make it worth reading and we'll read it.

And if we like reading your newsletters and they don't waste our time, then you and your quals won't be strangers when it's time for us to review your submittal.

It's a clever way to tell us about your quals, your people, your projects and your approaches before an RFP ever comes out.

And best of all – it costs absolutely nothing!

Big impact, zero cost – clients and Selection Committees like things like that too.

NEWSLETTER January 2013

NOW WE ARE SIX

This month we celebrate six years in business! We could not have made it through these trying times without our wonderful clients and the good folks at the various cities who've helped get all the projects reviewed, approved and constructed.

2012 was our best year so far, and with the recession now behind us, and in spite of continued Congressional dysfunction, we're looking forward to a banner year. We hope soon to have a big announcement to make, but for now – spoilers! Stay tuned.

WMD-CST

We're starting the new year off with a really big bang, or rather trying to prevent such a big bang. The US military has nationwide Civil Support Teams (CST) trained at the ready in case of any incidents involving potential Weapons of Mass Destruction (WMD). Tasked to deploy at a moment's notice, they consist of highly-trained command, operations, communications, logistics, medical, laboratory and survey personnel.

In association with XXX Architects we will be providing all site civil analysis and design for Type IA and IB services for a new WMD-CST facility right next to the tarmac at a large regional airport. Let's hope these guys get all the expert training they could ever need, and then never have to actually use it.

[YOUR PROJECT HERE]

In business since 2007, XXX provides complete site civil engineering services from initial investigations through concepts and design and final construction, including all Large Scale Development and Planning Commission reviews and approvals.

As a small business we usually beat the larger firms on price, service and value, and we'd love to talk with you about providing civil engineering services for your current and upcoming projects. We work nationwide, and are currently licensed in XXX. For more information contact XXX.

SITE / CIVIL / PLANNING / INFRASTRUCTURE

Or make them come to you

Instead of sending out emails and newsletters, how about getting your clients to seek you out instead?

It's the hottest new trend in marketing today and it's called Content Marketing. It's harder than it sounds but the theory is if you provide valuable enough content then the world will beat a path to your door.

The content is usually free, online, and works to establish you as a Subject Matter Expert (SME) and go-to firm for valuable state-of-the-art professional information.

Most firms do it through blogs, websites and online forums, but there are many ways you can establish yourself as a leader in your field to the point where the marketplace takes notice.

How about posting videos online about an important topic in your field? Or write a blog, or host some webinars, or write some eBooks, or offer freely downloadable white papers? Ask to speak at professional society meetings and conferences. Write articles for various professional and trade publications.

If other professionals are taking advantage of the opportunity to learn something from your valuable insights and information, you can be sure that members of Selection Committees are also doing the same and also noticing your presence and expertise.

Offer something of real value. Build trust and build loyalty.

Create a strong, reliable and highly identifiable brand.

Make us hope you submit on our next RFP.

Leverage & learn

But what if you're just starting out and wanting to grow your business to where you can handle larger and more complex projects, but your quals aren't quite up to the task just yet?

How do you get the experience that is often required by the RFP and the Selection Committee?

Nobody starts out being able to qualify for multi-million dollar projects, but there are two ways to get there:

- **Time**
- **Teaming**

The first involves building your practice slowly over time, project by project, getting bigger and better each time.

The second grows your expertise and experience much faster through teaming and partnering with the right people.

There's absolutely nothing wrong with learning from larger firms. In fact, the Small Business Administration has a very active mentor/protégé program designed to do just that.

If you're small, many government clients would prefer you team with a larger firm. They like the comfort level of knowing you've got additional expertise and personnel in the wings if needed.

Of course, team wisely. Make sure it's a firm that plays fair and has a strong commitment to working well with smaller firms.

Larger projects often have Small Business/DBE/WOSB/SDVOSB/ 8(a) participation goals, so the larger firms actually need you to help them win the larger project.

And you need them to get access to bigger and better projects to build your qualifications.

Done right, everybody benefits.

From little pup to Big Dawg

An architectural firm I worked with, known mostly for smallish local and regional projects, was asked by a large nationwide firm to join their team as the local contact for an Army Aviation planning project at a major Air Force Base.

The project went well, the Air Force was pleased, and when the RFP for the design of the $30M facility came out another nationwide firm asked this same local architectural firm to join them due to their prior experience with the planning phase and the client. Again, another successfully completed project.

But guess who won the design award and got to prime the next project on that Air Force Base? The small local firm.

The client knew them, their capabilities and their past performance, and knew they could hold their own without needing a large mega-firm to back them up.

Large nationwide firms are now asking if they can be subconsultants to *them*.

If you're a small firm with little experience, learn from the Big Boys and make a name for yourself with the client.

Team strategically and never forget:

It's who you know gets you places, and what you know keeps you there.

Secrets of the Selection Committee

How agile are you?

There's a new game in town and its name is "Agile."

It's a revolutionary new process that focuses on close collaboration between clients and self-organizing teams, face-to-face communication, constant scope changes, early and continuous delivery of project value.

Originally developed by computer software developers, its core principles can also be adapted and applied to developing and managing a host of other kinds of projects.

The Agile Manifesto

Individuals and Interactions	over	Processes and Tools
Working Product	over	Comprehensive Documentation
Customer Collaboration	over	Contract Negotiation
Responding to Change	over	Following a Plan

That is, while there is value in the items on the right, we value the items on the left more.

If you hear people talking about project chartering, servant leadership, scrums, story points, sprints, refactoring, fast failure, time boxes, daily stand-ups, task boards, burn up charts, burn down charts, velocity and retrospectives – then you know they are conversant in this radical new project management style.

Clients are looking for the best product by the best team using the most modern techniques. Familiarity with Agile could put you head and shoulders above the conventional competition.

The 12 Agile Principles

1. Our highest priority is to satisfy the customer through early and continuous delivery.

2. Welcome changing requirements, even late in development. Agile processes harness change for the customer's competitive advantage.

3. Deliver working products frequently, from a couple of weeks to a couple of months, with a preference to the shorter timescale.

4. Business people and developers must work together daily throughout the project.

5. Build projects around motivated individuals. Give them the environment and support they need, and trust them to get the job done.

6. The most efficient and effective method of conveying information to and within a development team is face-to-face conversation.

7. Working products are the primary measure of progress.

8. Agile processes promote sustainable development. The sponsors, developers, and users should be able to maintain a constant pace indefinitely.

9. Continuous attention to technical excellence and good design enhances agility.

10. Simplicity – the art of maximizing the amount of work not done – is essential.

11. The best architectures, requirements, and designs emerge from self-organizing teams.

12. At regular intervals, the team reflects on how to become more effective, then tunes and adjusts its behavior accordingly.

YOUR PROPOSAL

Ok, now that you know the RFP, the evaluation criteria and your quals, simply distill it into a limited 2D assemblage of paper.

That is your quest.

Not entirely impossible, but if it's all the Selection Committee has to work from then it ought to be pretty damn good if you want to be selected.

Read and re-read the RFP. Again. Know it by heart.

Some RFQ's are free-for-alls, just "send what you got." Most, however, require you to follow specific formats, page limits, fonts and sizes, etc.

Whatever the format, always keep in mind that the goal of your proposal is to win the work. So it shouldn't be something taken lightly or thrown together hastily or sloppily.

You need to clearly and convincingly show how your people, experience and past performance makes you the most qualified firm to address our needs.

Never forget that your proposal forms a basis for someone else's decision-making.

If you want that decision to be in your favor then you need to make sure your proposal says what it needs to say in the most effective way possible.

Know the audience you're writing for and write for the decision makers in that audience.

Don't write too little, don't write too much. Just like the Baby Bear's porridge, make it "just right."

But first, have you done your homework?

What do you know about the <u>PROJECT</u>?

If the RFP is the first you've heard of it then you're already way behind the pack.

Like cramming for a test, you've now waited until the very last few weeks (or days) to do your research, assemble your team and write your proposal.

If you have questions about the project? Too bad. We can answer specific questions about the RFP itself, but once it hits the street we can't meet with you and talk about the project. If we do, then we have to issue an official addendum with the answers for everyone. So you've lost any advantage you might have had by meeting with us privately beforehand.

You need to learn how to get in front of the RFP. Know what is coming up and when, and if you're a good fit. If you can learn what projects are coming down the pike and track them closely, then you can have your team and even a substantial portion of the proposal materials ready to go by the time the RFP is officially announced.

Many clients and most government agencies have Capital Improvement Plans (CIP) with estimated schedules and costs for all upcoming projects for the next 5 or so years. Sometimes this is published, sometimes not, but it behooves you to find out what projects are on the list, what is the estimated budget and when do they think the design phase is likely to be funded.

Before the RFP comes out you can usually meet with us and find out all the details and ask all sorts of questions. You'll learn things that might or might not make it into the official RFP wording, and you'll also have a chance to meet with us face-to-face and personally impress us with how qualified and interested you are in our upcoming projects.

What do you know about the <u>CLIENT</u>?

How well do you know how we work, how we think, our culture, our funding cycles, how we run our business? What about our protocols and procedures? What are our goals? What do we look for in a vendor/contractor? What are our hot buttons and pet peeves? Our constraints and stress points? What do we typically look for in a proposal? What problems have we had in the past that you could have prevented?

What do you know about the <u>INCUMBENT</u> (or the FAVORITE)?

What will it take to unseat them? What are their strengths? What are their weaknesses? Where do you excel where they don't? What do you know that they don't? Why are you better?

What do you know about the <u>COMPETITION</u>?

Who else is going after this? What are their strengths and weaknesses, past performance? How are you better?

What do you know about your <u>TEAM</u>?

Why are they your best support? What makes them your perfect complement? Special qualities? Special connections?

What do you know about <u>YOURSELF</u>?

Why are you the best firm for this client and this project? Why is your team the strongest? Why is your expertise a perfect match? Why is this a perfect project and perfect client for you? How do your experiences and your processes ensure project success? Are you up to the task at hand?

Finding your story

Written qualifications don't just magically appear – someone has to develop them by knowing what they're writing about.

Most firm's quals are written by a marketing department or a proposal coordinator and not the technical folks on the team.

Of course, your technical professionals should be involved in helping select the example projects, identifying key personnel and subconsultants, and the specific topics and issues that need to be addressed.

But don't expect them to write much proposal content – they probably don't have time and it's very likely out of their comfort zone anyway.

Give them a list of example projects to choose from, tell them to select their appropriate résumé projects (in order), and ask them for a paragraph or two for specific sections.

Better yet, give them an outline or a draft or a go-by that they can simply markup and edit. If you give them a blank sheet of paper and expect them to write the sections for you, you'll probably end up with a blank sheet of paper.

Consult with them on the Organizational Chart to make sure all disciplines are covered with the appropriate lines of authority.

Quiz them on key aspects, lessons learned, major successes.

Get them to tell you "what's the coolest thing about this project?" And where the really good photos are.

Give them plenty of time before the deadline to give you their ideas and their markups, stay after them until they deliver and then you'll have the tools to write a killer proposal that will impress the Selection Committee.

Follow ye rules, everyone. Every one.

Although it is possible to be selected even if a few pieces are missing, why take that chance?

- If the RFP asks for answers to specific questions, answer all, leave none out.

- If the RFP says to use a specific font and size, such as Arial 10pt or Times New Roman 11pt or 12pt, do it.

- If the RFP has a page limit, do not exceed.

- If the RFP has a submittal deadline, meet or beat it.

- If the RFP asks for organic soy-based ink on 100% recycled paper with chipboard folders bound with yarn made of Egyptian cotton hand-picked by happy school children, you must find a way to do it.

- If you disagree with any of the requirements of the RFP, do it anyway unless you want to risk getting tossed.

This is the crucial first test: "Can you follow directions?"

Standard forms

One of the most common proposal forms used in federal government work is known as Standard Form 330 (SF330) which replaced the previous Standard Form SF254/255 in 2004.

Many local governments modeled their forms after the old SF254's and SF255's so variations of the older format still exist.

SF330 – Part I

Sections A, B, C – Contract/POC/Team. Clearly identify the team and which branch office is doing the work.

Section D – Organizational chart. All bases covered, clear lines of authority, names of key personnel and all subconsultants.

Section E – Résumés. Make sure the proposed role matches the roles in the example projects, emphasize special training and relevant projects.

Section F – Projects. Similar size, issues & complexity.

Section G – Participation Matrix. Has the team worked together before and have they worked on the projects you're showing? Blackout Bingo is the goal.

Section H – Additional Information. Make your case, don't restate the obvious, answers all questions, bring it all home.

SF330 – Part II

A quick snapshot of core competencies and capabilities and employee counts plus principal signature.

Standard forms are designed to make everyone look alike. But that's the last thing you want, right?

Without getting too carried away, it's ok to improve the basic formatting, add colors, and even include graphics and photos where appropriate to try to personalize these impersonal forms.

SF330 Section H Checklist
USACE Louisville

1. Design Quality Management Plan
   a. Explanation of firm's management approach
2. Management of Subs
   a. Methods, techniques, approach
3. Quality Control Procedures for:
   a. Plans
   b. Specifications
   c. Design Analysis
   d. Electronic Documents
4. Design Quality Management Plan and various team components including subcontractors
5. Procedures to insure that internal resources are not over-committed
6. Organizational chart
   a. Show interrelationship of management and subs
7. Estimated percentage involvement for each
   a. Describe the type of work and roles each firm will play
8. Capacity to complete the work on time
   a. Show understanding that contract will require multiple design teams to work individual task orders at various locations simultaneously
9. Past performance on DOD projects
   a. Cost Control
   b. Quality of work
   c. Compliance with performance schedules
10. Extent of SB/DBE participation

The 12 most common proposal sections

PROFESSIONAL QUALIFICATIONS / FIRM CAPABILITIES

This is a general intro demonstrating why you are qualified for the proposed project. Briefly tell us what you're good at and why. This could conceivably be a standard paragraph that you include with each proposal.

SPECIALIZED EXPERIENCE

In this section we want you to show us what special skills or experience your team has that relate directly to the project in the RFP. This might be a standard boilerplate paragraph, but if so it should be specific to the type of project.

PROJECT UNDERSTANDING

This is not a regurgitation of the RFP Statement of Work, but it's where you tell us in your own words your understanding of the project along with any anticipated issues or challenges that will need to be addressed.

PROJECT APPROACH

This is the most important section in your entire proposal. We want to see how you propose to solve the problem at hand, what's your plan of attack, and what ideas and resources you will bring to bear to ensure a successful end result. Some firms even go so far as to generate conceptual designs and renderings of the project from the RFP. Yes, it's expensive to do that, but it can make a huge difference between you and everyone else.

ORGANIZATIONAL CHART

We're looking for coverage of all the major disciplines required by the project, which person or firm is responsible for what, with clear lines of authority delineated for each.

RÉSUMÉS

We'll be looking really closely at these, so make sure it's the team we'll see on the project if selected and make sure the roles shown for each person are similar or identical to the roles in the proposed project. We also want to know specifically what each person did on each referenced project in their résumé.

PROJECTS

These need to be relevant, similar size and complexity, and preferably in the same general geographic location as our project. Tell us your challenges, successes and lessons learned.

MANAGEMENT APPROACH

This is usually standard boilerplate material, customized if need be, to clearly show us how you will manage the scope, the costs, the schedule, the team, the quality and the client.

QA/QC PROGRAM

You need to tell us specifics about your QA/QC process and not give us a bunch of jive or generic nonsense. We want to know about your checks and balances (especially for subconsultants), plan review, timely responses, team coordination, anything and everything you do that will ensure a quality product for us.

PAST PERFORMANCE

We want concrete examples that show you've done this sort of work before and are perfectly capable of doing it again for us. This is a good place to include evaluations and testimonials.

CAPACITY AND WORKLOAD

We know you have other projects that you're working on so you need to tell us how ours would fit into your schedule and what you will do to make sure our project is never on the back burner. Execution is critical and we need to know you can do it.

OFFICE LOCATIONS

We want to know which office of yours will be doing the actual work and how close your people are to us and/or the project site. We know full well the problems associated with branch offices and outsourcing, so convince us that isn't a problem.

Make sure you answer these six classic questions clearly and concisely

WHO?   Company Description, Org Chart, Résumés

WHAT?   Project Understanding

WHERE?   Office Locations, Project Locations

WHEN?   Schedule

WHY?   Specialized Experience, Firm Qualifications, Projects, Past Performance

HOW?   Project Approach, Management Approach, Capacity, QA/QC

Match your quals to the RFP

I'm always amazed to see submitted proposals that have nothing whatsoever to do with the topic or qualifications asked for in the RFP.

Are some firms really that clueless? Or that lazy?

Do you really think your standard off-the-shelf quals are good enough to cover any eventuality and therefore don't need any tailoring to the specific RFP?

Or do you think throwing a useless submittal in front of us somehow endears us to you and keeps your name in front of us like a placeholder? We'll remember you all right, but not in the way you want.

I've also seen quals that were way overboard and beyond what the RFP was asking for.

Hey, do ya want the job, or not?

If the client wants you to design a city street, don't submit projects and photos of 8-lane freeways and large cloverleaf interchanges.

If the RFP asks for water and sewer line experience, don't include grading and paving projects.

If the RFP is asking for hospital and medical experience, don't include submarine docking facilities.

If the client wants a doghouse, don't give them the Taj Mahal.

All they wanted was a traffic light

A state highway department RFP for a rural intersection stated: "the purpose of the project is to improve traffic safety and increase the efficiency of the intersection by installing a traffic signal."

Couldn't be much more basic than that, right?

Well, one of the submittals was full of rainy day photos of the existing intersection (I'm pretty sure the DOT already knew what it looked like). Any photos of traffic signals anywhere in the proposal? Not a one, existing or proposed.

Résumés included an ADA Specialist (the project had no sidewalks), Community Planner (no planning needed), Utilities Engineer (no water or sewer utilities needed), Environmental Investigator (no environmental issues), and a Certified Floodplain Manager (no floodplain).

Any of the résumés mention traffic signals? Nope.

Any of the projects mention traffic signals? Nope.

The section titled "Anticipated Concepts and Alternative Methods" was answered with generic corporate bs and was totally devoid of any talk of concepts or alternates like roundabouts or other types of traffic management schemes.

Needless to say, they weren't selected.

Total fail.

Why did they even waste their time to submit?!?

Watch your language

Don't write with long-winded fancy prose like an English paper in high school and don't be too informal like a note or a text to a good friend or colleague.

Write simply, effectively, friendly and professionally.

Use high-impact words.

Short sentences.

Short paragraphs.

Bullet points.

Strive for 8th grade readability.

Make every word count towards the goal.

Avoid at all costs:

- bizspeak
- jargon
- excessive wordiness
- overly formal language
- passive tense
- convoluted sentences
- colloquialisms
- hyperbole
- platitudes
- clichés

Any idea what these examples from real proposals are trying to say?:

"Each of our projects that have been awarded from public agencies and private industry has been accomplished with completeness since the firm's inception."

"Successful project management requires a myriad of understanding peripheral to the project scope."

"The primary quality and efficiency tool is to keep the team intact through the life of the contract. This will allow the format, form and content of deliverables be consistent which minimizes time constraints."

> *"Write with such clarity and efficiency that reading your material is easy – even enjoyable."*
>
> Bryan A. Garner
> *HBR Guide to Better Business Writing*

Every sentence, every paragraph, every graphic, every photo should advance the narrative and bolster your case. If it doesn't do exactly that, throw it out. Be brutal. Be merciless. Hone and keep honing until it's loud and clear and unmistakable.

Remarkable and unforgettable are good, too.

Never forget **why** you are writing the proposal in the first place.

Your proposal is not a writing assignment

It is a targeted document that builds the case for why you are the best and most qualified firm to win the specific project.

Everything you write or present should reinforce this basic premise.

Anything that does not reinforce the premise should be rigorously omitted.

Active or passive?

One of the biggest mistakes you can make in your writing is to couch everything in passive tense instead of active tense.

Think about it, would you want to hire someone who is active or someone who is passive? The language in your proposal can create either impression so it's vitally important to search for and root out any and all language that does not portray you in the most active way possible.

Writing in the passive voice puts a distance between you and the reader while writing in the active voice creates a more dynamic personal connection that focuses on you.

Passive voice emphasizes the action.

Active voice emphasizes the actor.

PASSIVE: The project was designed by XXX.

ACTIVE: XXX designed the project.

PASSIVE: All of our projects have been LEED certified.

ACTIVE: All our projects are LEED certified.

PASSIVE: New designs were proposed.

ACTIVE: We proposed new designs.

WORDS TO WATCH OUT FOR: was, were, have been.

Keep it simple

There were two speeches at the dedication of the Soldiers National Cemetery in Gettysburg, PA, in 1863. Edward Everett's oration contained 13,607 words and lasted over two hours. Abraham Lincoln's address had only 227 words in ten sentences and was over in two minutes.

Which one does everyone still remember **150 years later**?

Does anyone remember *anything* about Everett's speech???

If you give us page after page of excessive and unfocused text with no paragraphs and tiny margins and no photos, I can guarantee you no one is going to read it. No one. Ever. Not even the person who finds it later in the trashcan where it belongs.

Don't tell yourself you're just being thorough by giving us a giant buffet of everything you can possibly think of – instead you're giving us unwanted indigestion and wasting our time.

You know the boor at the party who boxes you into a corner and then talks incessantly for hours only about themselves? That's you. That's your proposal. Do you know what we are thinking? SHUT UP ALREADY!!!

Instead,

"Should we hire you?"

> *"Yes"*

"Why?"

> *"Expertise, proven track record, best value"*

Convey this simple message with your words and photos.

The fewer the better.

Could you win a project with a poem?

An architectural firm in Las Vegas had been tracking a very important $250M project for some time but when the RFP came out it listed all sorts of criteria that they knew they couldn't fulfill.

So what did they decide to do?

Write a long evocative poem about the project instead.

Seriously.

Did they follow any of the RFP requirements?

Nope.

And guess what?

They won.

With no shortlist and no interview.

Instead of appealing to the client's head, as most proposal submittals do, their poem appealed to the client's heart. And that made the sale.

It might never happen again in the history of RFP's and proposals, but it did happen once.

If you're going to go rogue, go big.

The Dangers of Cutnpasteosis

Ok, raise your hands, how many of you routinely use cut and paste to grab sentences, paragraphs, graphics, charts, photos and even entire sections from previous proposals? I thought so.

Cut and paste is an amazing way to quickly copy text and graphics from one document to another.

It can be a great tool and it can be a real time saver.

It's also an amazing way to totally screw up if you don't pay attention and proofread everything thoroughly. It can mess you up big time.

I've seen it happen more than once. Great big gobs of stuff that were previously carefully tailored for one specific client, copied into a new proposal for a completely different client – totally unchanged.

The sweetest part is where the proposal talks about what an excellent QA/QC program you have... Yeah right.

You have to check exhaustively for typos, misspellings, crazy gibberish, non-sequiturs, miscellaneous garbage, and out-of-whack client and project references.

"Text Search" is your friend. Use it often and religiously to flush out bogus references and any and all vestigial junk left over from mindless cut & paste.

Right proposal, wrong client

In working on an annual SOQ to submit to a particular state agency, I asked the Marketing Coordinator of a firm where I once worked if she could get me a copy of what the firm had submitted the previous year.

Always good to know what we said last time. And who knows, maybe just make a few tweaks and resubmit.

Except...

In this instance Section H of the SF330 had obviously been cut and pasted wholesale from a totally different proposal. Instead of mentioning the current client it referred to a completely different government agency – *25 times!*

Hmmmm, no wonder the company never got any work from the previous SOQ...

Are you drowning in a sea of numbers?

This is an actual Table of Contents from a USACE document:

1.0 QUALITY CONTROL
    1.1 Purpose
       1.1.1 Project Scope
    1.2 References
    1.3 Responsibilities
    1.4 Basis of Design
       1.4.1 Consultants
    1.5 Methods
       1.5.1 Quality Reviews
       1.5.2 Design Checklist
       1.5.3 Quality Control Plan Monitoring
       1.5.4 Record Keeping and Filing

Or is something like this a little easier to read:

QUALITY CONTROL
    Purpose
       Project Scope

    References
    Responsibilities
    Basis of Design
       Consultants

    Methods
       Quality Reviews
       Design Checklist
       Quality Control Plan Monitoring
       Record Keeping and Filing

You're thinking you are being much more precise and organized doing it with specifications-style numbering but in reality the end result has exactly the opposite effect for the reader.

Use creative wayfinding and graphics instead of numb-ers.

Make things easy to read – *and* – easy to find at a glance..

Look at yourself

Take a good, long, impartial look at your proposal. Does it look professional? Does it convey the level of quality you espouse in the text?

Format good? Fonts good? Graphic and photos look good?

What about your résumé photos?

Do you look like someone you would want to work with, or do you look like a bunch of stiff dead presidents?

Not everyone is going to be fashion-model-photogenic, but I've seen résumé photos that would scare horror movie producers. And ones that would put a brick to sleep.

If the résumé and photo is all the Selection Committee has to go by to decide if they can trust and rely on your people, then do everything you can to make them look as good as possible and reflect their skills and personality.

Engage the services of a professional photographer if need be – it will be money well spent.

Same for your projects. A few killer photographs could mean the difference between being noticed and being passed over.

If your submittal is electronic only, double check how it looks on screen with different browsers, tablets, and even smartphones.

Appearances are important. If your proposal looks professional and organized, then there's a good chance we'll think you are too.

If you need help with graphic design, study Robin Williams' excellent *Non-Designer's Design Book.*

The handwriting on the wall

A friend of mine at NAVFAC Pacific told me they once got a SF330 submittal that was handwritten.

Handwritten!?!

Seriously, how in the world could anyone think that was appropriate or professional, or would have even a snowball's chance in hell of success?

I know it's recommended that you personalize your proposal as much as possible, but that's probably taking it a bit too far.

It's OK to show some personality

Preferable even.

Do you have any idea how boring most of your company descriptions and résumés are?

Spice them up a bit if you can, or add some inserts or photos that will catch a reviewer's attention.

Give us something we'll remember that directly relates to our project and our needs.

We want to know who you are, how you think.

Perhaps even something like this:

We are

Paddlers, Hula Dancers, Musicians

What does this have to do with architecture or engineering or whatever? Lots.

- ◆ Dedication
- ◆ Teamwork
- ◆ Coordination
- ◆ Strength
- ◆ Creativity
- ◆ Cooperation
- ◆ Community

All kine good things to have on your project, yeah?

Tell a story that is compelling and memorable

No, not the one about your kid in summer camp, or the time you found yourself lost in the back streets of Paris or Podunk.

The dramatic story you need to tell is how you've successfully responded to and handled obstacles and challenges on similar projects for similar clients. Simple as that.

Your story should check all these boxes if at all possible:

- ✓ Expertise
- ✓ Experience
- ✓ Approach & Methodology
- ✓ Innovation
- ✓ Performance
- ✓ Schedule
- ✓ Cost
- ✓ Quality
- ✓ Client Satisfaction

And if you make that story interesting to follow by making it unfold like an exciting novel or screenplay, then you'll be giving the Selection Committee something to remember you over all the other applicants who are probably droning on with endless boring facts.

Facts may speak to the head, but stories speak to the heart.

Make sure your story is something that you (or anyone else) would want to read, both in subject and in style.

But don't write the story you want to tell...

...write the story we need to hear.

"Stories are the new data."

Craig Galati
LGA Architects, Inc.

The Case of the Missing Elephant

Torrential rains and flooding were preventing vehicles of any type from moving some critical geotechnical drilling equipment from one job site to another on a large project in Thailand.

So, what do you think the American engineering firm in charge of the project did?

They hired a man with elephants to get the job done. *Yes, elephants.*

Is that the most awesome story EVER about doing whatever it takes to get the job done or what?!?

Can *any* other firm even come close to matching that story?

But for all the time I worked for that company they never mentioned it in any of their marketing or proposals or presentations. Never.

Now, if I were a reviewer reading through stacks of sameness and saw something that said:

"We'll do whatever it takes to ensure project success – we've even hired elephants"...

Whoa! Now *that* would grab my attention!

I'd immediately want to know who are these guys? And more about their creative thinking and resourcefulness.

What a hugely missed opportunity to really stand out from the crowd.

Elephants! That's a story we'd never forget.

White space is not your enemy

Doesn't it just hurt sometimes to leave any empty space on the page when you could be cramming it full of more text or details or graphics proclaiming your excessive wonderfulness?

I've seen pages with less than ¼" margins, single-spaced with no spaces between paragraphs or bullet points and sometimes with not even separate paragraphs and often justified all over like the awful text on page 15.

Seriously, do you think anyone is going to take the time to slog through all that? No one wants to drown in an endless sea of text that is completely unreadable. So why do you do it?

If you wanted to get the point across that you have consistently completed 30% plans in 30 days and that you provide quick and excellent customer service, how about doing it like this instead:

Our promise to you: 30% plans in 30 days.

Did all that white space kill you? Or did it make you take notice?

And your point is?

For every statement and every graphic in your proposal, ask yourself this simple question:

"So what?"

Or be like the little toddler who questions everything:

"Why?"

If you don't know why you've put the various things into your proposal, then consider tossing them out as superfluous at best and harmful at worst.

Make sure everything (words, graphics, photographs, even formatting) works toward the common goal of demonstrating beyond a doubt why you should win the project.

Don't ramble, don't pile on unnecessary fluff. Don't do the typical proposal barf. Make your point and make it as strong and convincing as possible.

> **"Trim the fat!"**
> **"Cut the crap!"**
>
> If this isn't your battle cry, it should be.

Back up all claims

If I only had a nickel for every time I've read or heard...

"We are leaders in (fill in the blank)"

"We have extensive experience in (fill in the blank)"

...almost never followed by anything even remotely resembling backup or proof.

Most proposals are chock-full of unsubstantiated claims, some more preposterous than others, some even laughable.

If you're going to make bold statements, you'd better be able to back up all of them – "show me" or else.

- "On time and on budget" – when, where, how much?

- "We are leaders in ....." – says who?

- "We are client-centered" – how?

- "many," "various," "numerous" – when, where?

It's ok to make assertions that highlight your experience and skills, but *always* show how they benefit the client.

Statements and claims don't win the job. But demonstrating the benefits of those statements will help you win every time.

"We do everything"

Oh really? Seriously?

How many times have you heard a firm say that?

How many times has YOUR firm (or you) said that?

And what does that mean, exactly?

> Do you pump septic tanks? (Probably not).

> Do you pluck chickens? (Probably not).

> Do you sell crack on the street corner (???)

Better to sharpen your focus and talk about the specific things you do best. Maybe 5 or 6, tops.

Make sure everyone (especially the Selection Committee) knows exactly what you excel at.

Everything? Sure, give me three. In what colors?

Give us the team we're getting

Of course everyone wants to showcase their A-Team and every client wants that same A-Team on their project.

But don't pull résumés from all over to try to look more impressive by presenting your top personnel regardless of location when you have no intention of actually assigning them to the project if you win it.

Show us good people, but only the good people who would actually work on our project.

This is especially true when it comes to the Shortlist Interview. Bring the same folks who were in the proposal.

We want to know how the people standing in front of us think and work. And we fully expect to see them again if we give you the project.

Bait & Tackle or Bait & Switch?

Some firms, no matter how large, include the résumés of their top employees for every submittal, thinking that's the way to look the strongest. No matter if these people are scattered all over the country, or the globe, and have probably never worked together.

Luckily, most clients are now wise to this after noticing they weren't seeing these personnel on the project after it was awarded.

After receiving submittals for a large sanitary sewer system RFP several years ago, the City of Houston let it be known that they expected to see the same personnel on the job site that were in the proposal, and if any firms wanted to resubmit they were welcome to.

Almost everyone did!

Show us your wrangling skills

Subconsultant coordination is a far greater task than many firms pay attention to or adequately address in their submittals.

We know you probably don't do everything yourself, so that's why you've assembled such a great team of supplementary and complementary experts, right?

But if a sub fails in the submittal, or the interview, or the project, that's your fault as the prime. You are the captain of the ship and we look to you to make sure everyone works well together for a successfully completed project.

- Tell us how you select and vet your subs.

- Tell us why you picked the subs for this submittal.

- Tell us how you've worked together previously.

- Tell us how you coordinate and manage their work.

- Tell us how you handle conflicts and discrepancies.

- Tell us why the sum is greater than the parts.

- Tell us why it gives us better value and better success.

Make sure we like your team members and that there have been no previous issues with their people or their work. Don't let a faulty team member sink your chances.

How you gonna manage all that?

In an attempt to cover all the positions and bases listed in the RFP, a firm I worked for once included 27 subconsultant companies on the org chart.

27 !!!

Needless to say it was a nightmare trying to round up all the qualifications from so many firms for the proposal. It made herding cats look really easy.

Company info, résumés, projects, logos, etc.

No matter what was in the data call to every team member, not everyone responded promptly.

Not everyone sent everything that was requested.

Not everything was in the requested format.

So how smoothly do you think it will go if you win the project and have this many firms on board?

The Selection Committee is thinking the same thing.

A cast of thousands is a huge red flag. Different accounting systems, different billing cycles, different review procedures, etc. Where's the proof they can all play well together?

Instead, consider teaming with a large firm who has all (or most of) the capabilities you need. That will give you a single point of contact plus instant depth in your bench from a single capable and proven source.

Show us how you manage these 6 basic things

1. SCOPE

2. SCHEDULE

3. COST

4. CLIENT

5. TEAM

6. QUALITY

Gratuitous graphics & phancy photographs

Photos and graphics should be relevant and should support and enhance, not distract. Don't just stick something on the page because there's a blank spot or because you think it's pretty.

"Every picture tells a story."

Roderick David Stewart, CBE

What stories do your pictures tell? And your graphics?

Every single photo should reflect who you are, what you've done, and how well you understand the client and their needs.

Every photo should be as carefully selected as any text.

Select for relevance, quality and impact.

If a picture is truly worth a thousand words, spare the long-winded text and show some demonstrative photographs or infographics instead that are real attention-grabbers.

If appropriate, also include visually impressive charts and graphs and other visuals to dramatically make your points.

But don't get carried away unnecessarily. Avoid pointless photos and over-abundant or distracting graphics.

Instead, use photos, color, text blocks, highlighting, different fonts and other creative wayfinding elements to help a reviewer quickly find and understand your key points.

Battleships on the Battlefield

A state Department of Defense whose divisions included the Army National Guard, Air National Guard, Civil Defense and Disaster Preparedness Divisions put out an annual call for Statements of Qualifications.

The Publications Department of the company I worked for created a fancy proposal cover that prominently featured a full-page photograph of the famous battleship USS Missouri.

Internal dividers included photos of aircraft carriers and major naval facilities.

Too bad the National Guard doesn't have a navy.

Or any battleships. Or aircraft carriers. Not anywhere in the 54 states and territories.

What message would this have sent to the members of their Selection Committee?

"We have no idea what you do but hire us anyway."

Past performance

I'm always surprised how many firms really fall down on this section. This is not the place to rehash previous corporate bs, but the place to tell us about your successes.

Don't just say "on time and on budget" – give us a chart showing some real dates and numbers.

Don't just say "the project was successful" – give us some quotes from key client stakeholders.

> *"Complications arose, ensued,*
> *were overcome."*
>
> Capt. Jack Sparrow

Include a brief summary of your successes, challenges met and lessons learned.

You consistently design to the budget? Tell us.

Your cost estimates are within 2% of construction costs? Tell us.

Prove to us beyond a shadow of a doubt that you've done it before and you can do it again for us.

Experience is WHAT you have done.

Past performance is HOW WELL you did it.

Past Performance Criteria

(HDOT)

Hawaii Department of Transportation

- Project title, location, year completed and scope.

- Client's name and phone number.

- Client's primary project manager or contract administrator.

- Successful project elements.

- Project challenges and how they were overcome.

- How successes or lessons learned can apply to this contract.

The Power of Praise

Short, strong, relevant, positive quotes from influential people you've worked for are far more compelling than simply listing their names and addresses as references.

If someone on the Selection Committee actually knows any of the people who are praising you that's worth its weight in gold.

If you've received positive evaluations on previous projects, include excerpts.

Plus any positive press or articles in magazines, newspapers and trade journals.

Awards are good, too. Everyone prefers to work with a winner.

The words of others will speak volumes louder than anything you could write yourself.

Check, reread, proofread. Everything. Repeat.

Contrary to what you might think, spellcheckers are not your friend. They make you lazy and codependent.

They make it way too easy for errors to slip through, only to be caught by the very folks you're trying to impress.

Sorry, but you can't fix this one by pushing a button. You've got to do it old school by deliberately reading every single word, singly.

And every sentence, sentencely.

And every paragraph, paragraphically.

So go ahead and use your spellchecker, but know that it's only a very rough first pass through your document that may or may not find errors.

But proofreading is not just about spellchecking – it's about checking everything from format to appearances to make sure it's exactly as you intend. It's always advisable to do a quick flip-through of every page before it goes out the door to make sure:

- ✓ All formatting, tabs and sections in proper order
- ✓ Pages, photos, tables, figures printed correctly
- ✓ No inadvertent, out of place or upside down pages
- ✓ All RFP issues addressed and questions answered
- ✓ Résumés match the Org Chart
- ✓ All "T's dotted and I's crossed"
- ✓ Correct mailing label

Make sure the client's name is spelled correctly. Everywhere.

Ladle Rat Rotten Hut*

If you rely solely on spellcheckers and autocorrect to catch all spelling errors, then you definitely need to read Howard Chace's amazing book *Anguish Languish* (Prentice-Hall, 1956).

Created as a work of humor using what is known as homophonic transformation, he rewrote well known stories and poems by substituting completely different words that sounded like the original words.

For the story in the title of this text box, the moral (or in his words, the "mural") is: "Yonder nor sorghum stenches shut ladle gulls stopper torque wet strainers."

Say it quickly and you'll figure out how it works.

But here's the clincher:

SPELLCHECKERS WOULD SAY THIS IS PERFECTLY OK!!!

Every single word in Chace's book would make it past every spellchecker with flying colors.

You need to read your proposal and not just trust your built-in spellchecker. For best results, read it out loud.

For best results, have a third party read and proofread.

You cannot check and proofread too much.

* Little Red Riding Hood

Proof your photos, too

The first test should be for relevance. Does every photo support your arguments, or do they just take up space?

Do the photos have high impact and command attention?

Check for layout, contrast, cropping and effects. Make sure it all looks good. Poor quality photos should be replaced or deleted.

Beware of overuse of fancy borders and excessive photo effects. If they detract from the message of the photo, minimize or remove. Some firms spend untold hours adding rounded corners, or shadows, or cheesy borders without realizing their time would be much better spent getting better photos.

Check for pixelation. Just because it looks good on your computer monitor is no guarantee it will look good in print. Monitors are typically 72 dpi (dots per inch) but you'll need at least 200 dpi for print. If you have any doubt, print out some test pages and verify your photos look sharp.

Check to make sure the photos show projects your firm actually worked on.

No generic stock photos, and no photos of competitor's projects (yes, I've seen it happen).

Scratch that

The corporate office of one firm I worked for sent out a batch of photos to be used for marketing.

But I'm pretty sure no one checked them before sending. At least I'm hoping that was the case.

Front and center of one very nice project photo was an unsuspecting individual who just so happened to be scratching his butt big time. Shirt raised up, hand down pants, exposed skin. You get the picture.

Make that: "we shouldn't have gotten that picture."

Embed thy fonts

Know what an embedded font is. Know how to do it. And know what can happen if you don't.

This: 𝔥arrington decorative font

Becomes: `Courier not so decorative font`

For printed materials it's not an issue but it can be huge for anything electronic.

It can happen to your MS Word documents, your pdf's, and it can happen to your slides and PowerPoints.

Of course it looks fine on your computer but if our computer has a different font set that doesn't include the special fancy fonts you worked so hard to find and use to create your own unique *fontastic* identity, you're in for a very big and very public surprise.

For printed documents, substituted fonts can instantly make all your formatting go kablooie.

Same thing for PowerPoint presentations – there's nothing like finding out too late when it's on the screen in front of the committee.

At that point all you can do is look stupid and unprepared. Which you are.

Far better to turn off your PowerPoint immediately and wing it than to dig the hole any deeper.

Verify the format

Do you have a standard corporate format that you send out for every proposal? No matter if it's what the client wants or not?

Some RFP's have very specific requirements, others leave it up to you, but it's always better to check and see what format the client would like to receive it in.

Some want specific numbers of paper copies bound a certain way, some want CD's, some want emailed pdf's. Check first, and follow the rules to the letter.

If it's not in the requested format, it could be grounds for getting it tossed.

If the RFP specifies a particular font and size, make sure that's what you've used.

And don't forget page counts. If the RFP calls for a maximum page count, you must follow it exactly. Tabs and cover letters and standard forms like Certificates of Insurance are often not included in the count, but check and double check to make sure.

Pages over the count could render the entire proposal non-compliant, or we might just toss everything after the stated number of pages. Either way you lose.

Save yourself and themself some trouble

For a US Army Corps of Engineers submittal a few years ago I called the contact number on the RFP to verify the best format for the submittal.

The guy who answered the phone told me he was the one who processed the submittals and that he was the one who went to the copy machine to make 19 copies for the reviewers, and that he threw all extraneous information in the trashcan beside the copy machine.

What would make his job easier? He suggested no bindings, no staples, no brochures, no oversized covers – just paperclip everything together.

The moral: Always check to make sure your submittal is in the format preferred by the client. No need to fill up their dumpster unnecessarily.

Latest software or most compatible software?

If you're making an electronic submittal, then you need to make sure you're sending files that the recipient can open.

Due to long procurement cycles and occasional bureaucratic ineptitude, government agencies often have software that is one or two versions back from what is current. So if you send files in the most recent format they might not be able to open them. Not good!

This was a huge problem when Microsoft Office went from .doc to .docx, and .xls to .xlsx, and it could easily happen again.

Find out what software the client uses and verify the version.

This is especially important for PowerPoint presentations if you're using features only found in the latest release – otherwise who knows what will be substituted instead?

If the RFP asks for pdf's, don't send documents in MS Word or InDesign (.indd) formats. Don't include project schedules in .mpp, or PowerPoints in .ppt or pptx.

If we can't open your files, they won't be opened.

If submitting by email, make sure to verify the file size capacity of our email server. If your final proposal file is too big it will bounce back as undeliverable. Also not good.

You might be surprised just how much bloat can creep into your files, from uncompressed photos to stray hidden junk lurking in the formatting codes. Compress, excise and clean as best you can without losing quality.

And last but not least, make sure your submittal looks good on screen with different browsers and on various tablets and smartphones to make sure we are seeing it exactly as you formatted it.

Downsaved or deleted

The architects at one place where I worked were very proud of always having the latest software and latest file formats, and they didn't care if anyone else (including clients and Selection Committees) could open the files or not.

It was almost like it was the client's fault for not having the latest and greatest software.

And even though clients had to repeatedly request them to downsave and resend that only seemed to reinforce their sense of superiority.

There's nothing wrong with having the latest software but if you care about making things easy for your client you should always save files in the formats that work best for them. Instead of irritating them or pissing them off or making their life more difficult.

My computer had an earlier version of AutoCAD that was incompatible with what they were sending. I got tired of their attitude and having to constantly ask them to downsave, so I finally told them I would just delete anything they sent if I couldn't open it.

I wonder how many clients (or Selection Committees) did the same thing?

Show everything but not everything

Don't send electronic files without first editing or cleaning them of everything non-essential or anything you don't want to share with the whole world.

Purge unneeded layers in AutoCAD, delete irrelevant text, columns, rows or extra worksheets or pages of notes that only you care about.

Don't send spreadsheets with hidden columns or rows. Or with broken links. Double check every formula and calculation to make sure they are ironclad and calculate as intended.

And never ever hide data in a spreadsheet by using white text in white cells. I once spent hours trying to find out why a long cost estimate didn't add up, only to eventually discover extraneous leftover numbers concealed in harmless-looking supposedly empty cells.

If you're submitting documents in Microsoft Word make sure the dreaded "Track Changes" tab is completely off, deactivated and completely sorted out or we'll get a document with a blown format and with all your messy internal notes off to the side.

Submitting in MS Word is fairly risky since it's a file that is easily editable by anyone else. If an RFP asks for it, call and see if you can submit PDF's instead.

Make sure all layers of PDF's are flattened, fonts are embedded and that everything has converted properly and your intended format is still intact.

As with everything you submit, make sure your electronic data is clean, concise, and only shows what you want the client to see and nothing else.

Things that will get your submittal noticed

- Professional look and feel, consistent style

- All RFP questions clearly answered

- Easy-to-read text and bullet points

- Interest-grabbing narrative & approach

- A-Team with strong subs

- Meaningful graphics

- Quality photos

- Strong references with quotes or scorecards

- Excellent past performance

- Something special and memorable

- Something that shows us your "wow" factor

- Something that gives us confidence in your abilities

- Something that shows you "get it"

- Something a winner would submit

How fit are you?

These slogans from the walls of my local fitness facility can also apply to your proposals:

- Make a DIFFERENCE
- GIVE it your all
- Exceed all EXPECTATIONS
- CHANGE your life
- Push your LIMITS
- BELIEVE in yourself
- Not over until you've WON

Think seriously about hiring a couple of personal trainers – one for your proposals and one for your presentations.

Proposal fails

Even if your proposal doesn't get thrown out early on, it can still fail to win you the job.

It's a "Little Piggy" Proposal. Lots of "we" "we" "we" all the way home. All about you, nothing about us. Makes us wonder if you know anything about us at all. Or care.

It fails to get our attention. Don't give us the "same old same old." Make us want to read your proposal.

Not focused. Give us a purposeful message instead of a clueless sea of text.

Not readable. Avoid long, rambling or flowery sentences filled with arcane language that impresses no one. No tiny fonts, tiny margins or paragraphs with no breaks.

Not convincing. Clearly show us your stuff and what you're made of, how you think, how you work, how you react, what you do best.

Superfluous crapola. Don't include extra material we didn't ask for like brochures, catalogs, reports, flyers, blow-ins.

Boring filler. Please, no irrelevant or useless pages, paragraphs, photographs or long-winded company histories.

Nothing why. You need to clearly answer The Question:

Why are you the perfect company for our project?

Things that will get your submittal tossed

- Late
- Incomplete
- Non-compliant
- Irrelevant
- Inappropriate
- Inaccurate
- Shoddy
- Disorganized
- Cluttered
- Excessive clichés
- Wild claims
- Errors & mistakes

The "5-second" test

One by one, give every page in your submittal a quick scan and take no more than 5 seconds to do it.

Did anything catch your eye?

Did the key points jump out?

Do you remember the gist of what the page is about?

Did anything make you think "wow"?

Did anything make you think "yuck"? Or "ho-hum"?

Believe it or not, this is probably more time than the typical reviewer will spend on each page, so if your message isn't readily clear in 5 seconds, then you need to consider how best to re-write and re-present your information.

The same goes for your photos and graphics. Give them a quick 5-second glance:

Do they catch your eye and draw you in?

Do they add clutter or clarity?

Do they tell their own powerful story?

Do they enhance the information on the page?

Do they provide a welcome contrast to all the text?

Are they clear, concise, self-explanatory, striking?

Deliver it on time

Do I really need to say this?

Do you really think the submittal deadline is just a suggestion?

We don't care about traffic or FedEx schedules or printing problems or computer problems or security problems or wrong building problems or any other of the host of excuses you sometimes have for not making the deadline.

I've run through airports, driven like a maniac, waded in floods, and made mad dashes through buildings to beat the clock. Was it worth taking years off my life to do it? Probably not.

The smart thing is to submit a day or two early and have a backup plan just in case.

Just because FedEx says they'll get it delivered by 10:00am the next day, that's not a true guarantee. Sure, they'll give you your money back, but that lost proposal? No liability. Some deliveries just run late, and if your submittal is on that truck, too bad.

Don't just drop it off with anyone who happens to be sitting in the guard shack or the receptionist's desk. Make sure it gets to the right place.

Always call to make sure your submittal has been received, not by the mailroom, but by the person to whom it is addressed. If their own mailroom fails to get it to them on time, they may or may not allow it to be late. Don't count on it.

If it's really important, don't rely on FedEx or any courier or delivery service – hand-carry it yourself. And who knows, you might even get to meet the client, and in some instances can even furtively see who else has submitted.

For electronic submittals hit "send" well before the clock strikes. Big files can take a lot more time than you think to upload and then be received on someone else's computer.

The future?

What if you had to submit a *video* proposal?

Don't laugh. Or panic. But get ready, that day might arrive a lot sooner than you think.

Neither paper submittal nor oral presentation, but 100% video.

Think of the incredible freedom you'll have to showcase your staff, your projects, your talents, your office. Think of all the new and wonderful things you can do with a video.

Think of the completely different talent set you will need to pull it off successfully.

Add dynamic graphics? Of course.

How about a hip soundtrack? Sure, why not?

But if you fall into the trap of just putting some boring talking heads in front of the camera, droning on about blah blah blah, that ain't gonna cut it.

It's going to require a whole new level of creativity, and yes, that filmmaking degree you got back in college might finally prove useful!

I know an architectural firm that did a video submittal even though it wasn't asked for, and it was awesome.

They didn't win. Perhaps a bit too radical for that particular client?

But a member of the Selection Committee was so impressed he subsequently recommended and hired them for a whole slew of new projects nationwide.

Visual storytelling via video will be the Next Big Thing.

YOUR PRESENTATION

Assuming your submittal made the first cut you're no longer constrained or defined by pieces of paper. Which is a good thing since your paper proposal was most likely written by someone else (but hopefully with a lot of input from you).

But the presentation is now 100% you. This is your moment to really shine. And this is the Selection Committee's chance to talk face to face with you and the team you're proposing.

Shortlist presentations are very specialized performances with a very specific objective – to be the winning selection. Yet for many it is little more than a perfunctory trip through yet another PowerPoint hell.

There's a lot at stake. How you handle the interview is a strong indicator of how you'll handle the project.

And we're looking to see if you're who you say you are, and if you know what you say you know.

Your interview can happen in one of three ways:

1. Telephone

2. Video conference

3. In person

For a routine project, the interview might be conducted by a Selection Committee of one. For major projects you'll have several members attending, and for very significant projects you could conceivably be facing a roomful of reviewers and project owners and stakeholders.

So if you're no longer limited by 2D paper, why do so many presenters shackle themselves to canned slide programs like PowerPoint and Keynote, or artsy swoopy things like Prezi?

"I hate the way people use slide presentations instead of thinking. People who know what they're talking about don't need PowerPoint."

Steve Jobs

Like all good journeys, your presentation should have a beginning, a middle and an end. With luck (actually, with a lot of planning) you and the selection committee will end up where you want, hopefully something interesting and memorable happened in between, and no one was lost or left behind in the process.

It's the same kind of journey you embark on when creating a good story, or a screenplay, or even a set list for a band or a musical program. Your task is to steer the ship through charted and uncharted waters until everyone reaches the destination safely and on time and with lasting positive memories.

There will be highs, lows, boring bits, and hopefully thrilling bits. Like a good roller coaster ride, your job is to create the right rhythm through a sea of contrasting ideas, words, images and sounds.

Be prepared

The interview is not just a public speaking engagement or a rehash of the quals in your paper submittal – it's also a test of your leadership and organization and your ability to accomplish a task within a given time.

Good presenters are:

- enthusiastic
- knowledgeable
- organized
- on-point
- client-focused
- understandable
- articulate
- adaptable
- humorous
- charismatic

Learn how to use appropriate body language and vocabulary, and teach yourself to speak in a naturally varied tone of voice.

If you include visual aids, make sure they:

- create interest
- add impact
- save time
- help with retention
- show things that are difficult to express verbally

Spam Spam Spam Spam

The good folks at the University of Southampton in the UK have created this easy-to-remember (and very Monty Pythonesque) aide-mémoire to help you structure your presentation:

SITUATION

Consider the time, place and conditions.

PURPOSE

Why are you giving this presentation?

AUDIENCE

Skillful presentation is not public speaking, it is audience-oriented, the focus is on the audience's needs.

METHOD

Which methods will best accomplish the purpose?

Before you hit the stage

Be very careful about socializing with the client before the interview...

...especially if alcohol is involved!

All the obvious reasons apply, plus you don't want to leak any juicy details that could diminish the impact of your upcoming presentation.

Need we say that hangovers and presentations do not mix well?

Instead, put on your coach's hat and huddle up the team for a rousing pep talk and any last minute suggestions or instructions.

And then get well-fed and well-rested the night before the big show.

Know in advance where the interview will be held and make a dry run beforehand to familiarize yourself with routes, traffic, building location and parking. You don't want to start your Big Day frantically searching for where you're supposed to be.

Last-minute rushed rehearsals will do you more harm than good. If you don't know your material well enough by now it's too late.

Far better to spend your final hours or minutes before you go on in a state of focused relaxation.

Who is your audience?

It's not you. Although a lot of presenters act like they're talking to themselves in some sort of weird introverted personal conversation that excludes any intellectual or emotional involvement from those in the audience.

You need to know who you are addressing, why they are there, and why they would care about anything you say or show.

Your goal is to convince them to pick you over all the others. So why do you often do the exact same boring shtick that all the others are doing?

Laziness? Incompetence? Lack of Preparation?

None of these are good indicators of how you'll handle our project.

Your presentation is an example of your work product, as is your paper submittal. So spend the time and effort to make the most of your very limited window of opportunity to make the big win.

Keep in mind that different people have different learning styles. Some do better with text, some are more visual and others are more auditory. Have something for everyone.

If you can't connect with your audience, you are wasting everyone's time.

It's a show alright

- Show us you know us and our business.

- Show us you understand the project.

- Show us you understand our needs.

- Show us you understand our processes.

- Show us you know your stuff.

- Show us others trust and rely on you.

- Show us you can handle "whatever."

- Show us similar scenarios, similar successes.

- Show us how you think.

- Show us caveats and enhancements.

- Show us how you ensure quality.

- Show us how you control costs.

- Show us how you meet schedules.

- Show us how you manage subconsultants.

- Show us every key team member.

- Show us why we'd be fools to pick anyone else.

Your mission

PLANNING   Analyze the situation
Do your reconnaissance
Have intel
Know the players
Develop a plan
Have back up plans

READINESS   Know your core competencies
Ready your team
All equipment in working order
Rehearse and train
Everything and everyone mission critical
No excess baggage

EXECUTION   Have an objective
Have a course of action
Have a leader
Know the terrain
Know the friendlies
Mobilize all necessary resources
Maximize your assets
Select the best team
Assign tasks
Have each other's back, no one left behind
Deploy and execute efficiently
Focus on the goal
Engage and win over hostiles
Amplify strengths, neutralize weaknesses
Anticipate events
Risk management instead of risk aversion
Know what you need to do to win

CELEBRATION / DEBRIEF

10 basic presentation elements

Appearance

Intro

Speaking

Timing

Confidence

Team

Approach

Visuals

Big Finish

Q&A

"Wow, this is going to be interesting!"
or…"Here we go again"?

How do you typically start your presentations? With hemming and hawing, fumbled introductions, lame attempts at humor, perhaps a long drawn out recitation about your company's history?

Guess what? We don't care about any of that.

You've got about 2 minutes to capture our attention with compelling and meaningful information or else we'll end up just sitting there suffering while begging the clock to hurry up.

Former electrical engineer and master sales trainer Tim Wackel distills presentations down to three key issues:

1. What is the problem?

2. How are we going to fix it?

3. Why should you choose us?

What: the problem or the opportunity

How: our plan with our unique skills and approach

Why: the payoff you'll get for selecting us

So start your presentation with something fresh – not the same old same old that you and everyone else typically do.

Your stupid intro slide with the project title and your contact information? Trash it. Start instead with something that will excite or intrigue the Selection Committee.

Presentation triage

Tim Wackel has a great analogy to help you rethink the presentation of your presentation.

What if you had a serious health problem and had to go to the hospital?

Would you appreciate it if the doctor or nurse came up to you and introduced themselves and told you the history of the hospital and where they went to school and how many patients they had and how many doctors and nurses they had on staff and many other patients they'd treated and what diseases and illnesses they typically treat and what medicines they like and how happy they are that you came to their hospital?

I bet you'd rather they tell you what's wrong as quickly as possible and how they're going to fix it.

But the first way is how umpty-ump million presenters and PowerPoint users start their presentations every day.

Pity.

That approach needs to be put down immediately. Put it out of its misery, for mercy's sake.

What if public speaking makes you speechless?

For many folks it's almost a fate worse than death to have to speak in public. Add to this fear the pressure of winning or losing and for some it can be almost unbearable.

But you have to learn to channel that negative energy into positive energy – make it work for you instead of against you.

You do that by knowing your material inside out, upside down and sideways, and by knowing you're just sharing what you know and are good at. There really shouldn't be any pressure – if it's not a good fit then you don't want the job anyway.

Remember you're the smart ones who can solve the Selection Committee's problems. They are there to learn from you (not to scare you).

Fight fear with familiarity – familiarity with the material, the team, the format and the setting.

Schedule extra rehearsals and practice sessions to do everything you can to take the edge off the fear. Don't rehearse word-for-word – concentrate instead on the overall outline and the big concepts.

If you have any key team members who simply cannot cope but have a critical role on the team, then find a way to minimize their speaking role while still making them an important part of the presentation. Put them in charge of several key tasks to help take their mind off their fear.

Let someone strong take the lead and give well-defined minor roles to those less comfortable in the spotlight.

Penn & Teller found a way to make the magic work with one silent partner and so can you!

Visual aids, visceral aids?

Only 11 short years after Microsoft introduced the PowerPoint program in 1990, Angela Garber coined the now famous phrase:

"Death by PowerPoint"

Unfortunately, it is still as true as ever.

PowerPoint was designed to be a huge leap forward from blackboards, overhead projectors, white boards, flip charts, and hand-drawn or typeset slides. But...

PowerPoint presentations have become the easy drug of choice since they are easy to create. Too easy.

And I use the word "create" very loosely. Simply throwing a bunch of crap into a standard template is not being creative. Making it interesting and effective – that's the challenge.

If you use PowerPoint slides for your presentations, you need to ask yourself these two questions first:

Where's the Power?

What's the Point?

Instead of inflicting a death-by-a-thousand-slides to your client, put some serious effort into understanding what slides are and are not capable of, and how they should enhance instead of detract from your core message.

Presentation slides are a visual medium and should be used to present visual concepts, not great big gobs of hard-to-read text.

"A slide's value is determined not by the amount of information it contains, but by how clearly it communicates its message."

– Nancy Duarte, *Slide:ology*

Presentation slides are:

- not a script
- not a document
- not a data dump
- not a cudgel
- not a sleep aid

Do you feel in your gut that your visual aids are killing it, or do you feel sick to your stomach that your visual aids are killing you?

If you're not happy with your visual aids, why inflict them on us?

So promise me right now that you will make every effort to find novel and interesting ways to visually present your main points and power your story to a winning presentation.

Avoid at all costs:

- Too much text
- Text too small
- Overly busy/illegible charts and graphics
- Trite or overused clipart
- Annoying cutesy transitions
- Slides left over from previous presentations
- Monotone slide reading

If you must use slides, there are several excellent books you should to study to dramatically improve your PowerPoint style: Alexei Kapterev's *Presentation Secrets*, Nancy Duarte's *Slide:ology* and *Resonate*, and Garr Reynolds' *Presentation Zen*.

Would you drink that?

Visual aids can be a lot more than just PowerPoint slides. For a presentation on water treatment I only needed three large glasses of water to get the point across.

The first glass was filled with water straight out of a muddy bayou, complete with leaves, twigs and God-knows-what else washed in from the storm sewers. "Anybody want to drink this?" A resounding "NO!" and looks of disgust from everyone in the room.

The second glass had water taken from the mixing chamber of a water treatment clarifier. Shaken up at the start of the talk, it had slowly settled into a layer of sediment at the bottom and a layer of fairly clear water at the top. Although offered, nobody wanted a drink of this one either.

The third glass contained water from the pipe leaving the water treatment plant, essentially basic everyday tap water – the visible and tangible result of the chemical and mechanical processes required to convert nasty bayou water into drinking water. When offered the opportunity to drink the water out of this glass, there were no takers. The description of the crud in that first glass of water must have been a little too graphic!

But imagine everyone's astonishment when I picked up that third glass and took a nice long satisfying drink.

The audience will not long forget that shocking visual image and demonstration of personal trust in the water treatment process we were proposing.

Pointing to your Points

Instead of a shaky handheld laser pointer and a stationary laptop, consider switching to an electronic pen and tablet for your presentations.

You're in more direct control and it's also much more dramatic to carry around your presentation with you as you walk around.

But best of all, it's much more effective since you can use the pen to highlight, underline, notate or circle the very things you're talking about at that very moment in real time.

I first saw this technology used to great effect over ten years ago – why is anyone still using wibbly wobbly laser pointers???

Better TED than dead

By now, everyone's heard of TED and TEDx presentations, right?

Created in 1984 as a one-off event by architect and graphic designer Richard Saul Wurman, it has morphed into a global phenomenon. Although initially focused on Technology, Entertainment and Design (TED) it now encompasses talks on a wide variety of topics that are "Ideas Worth Spreading."

Each TED speaker only has 18 minutes to present his or her idea in the best and most imaginative way possible. That's it.

TED.com has become an online source for several thousand TED Talks. Locally sponsored TEDx events have posted over 30,000 videos online from over 130 countries and TED Talk videos have been viewed over a billion times.

Why do I bring this up? Because these are some of the best presentations ever and you can watch many of them for free.

This ain't your father's Toastmasters.

Although Toastmasters has done a world of good for public speaking over the years, the TED talks have dramatically reinvigorated and reinvented public presentations.

So what does this have to do with your interview presentation?

A lot more than you think.

Although you have more information to present and more personnel to introduce than the typical TED speaker, you can learn from their engaging presentation styles how to hone your message to the barest and most effective essentials.

Notice how they introduce their topic, develop their story, and then close with a big finish. To great applause.

You need to be doing the exact same thing in order to win over a Selection Committee.

The TED Commandments

Thou Shalt Not Simply Trot Out thy Usual Shtick.

Thou Shalt Dream a Great Dream, or Show Forth a Wondrous New Thing, or Share Something Thou Hast Never Shared Before.

Thou Shalt Reveal thy Curiosity and Thy Passion.

Thou Shalt Tell a Story.

Thou Shalt Freely Comment on the Utterances of Other Speakers for the Sake of Blessed Connection and Exquisite Controversy.

Thou Shalt Not Flaunt thine Ego. Be Thou Vulnerable. Speak of thy Failure as well as thy Success.

Thou Shalt Not Sell from the Stage: Neither thy Company, thy Goods, thy Writings, nor thy Desperate need for Funding; Lest Thou be Cast Aside into Outer Darkness.

Thou Shalt Remember all the while: Laughter is Good.

Thou Shalt Not Read thy Speech.

Thou Shalt Not Steal the Time of Them that Follow.

Never-Never Land

Never read your presentation. Or your slides.

People read faster than you speak.

If you have slides with lots of text, what are you doing while everyone is sitting there reading instead of listening to you?

If everyone is reading *then you're unnecessary.*

If you ever have to stop and say "where was I?" — the obvious answer is "nowhere."

Instead of Presenter, you've just demoted yourself to Slide-Clicker. Audience engagement goes to zero. And no one wants to hire a menial Slide-Clicker.

Never turn your back to the Selection Committee. Or talk to the screen behind you.

In the world of theater, staging is incredibly important and it can be critical to your success in front of a Selection Committee.

Think of the area in front of the committee as your stage, with the screen as your backdrop and with your cast members ready in the wings.

- **Full Front** is the operative term.

- Use theater-style **blocking**.

- **Turn out** means always face the audience.

Seriously think about hiring a theater coach to train your team. You want to avoid a tragedy at all costs.

Never hide behind a podium, or fidget, or rattle your keys in your pocket, or mumble, or be distracted, or be...

- Unprepared

- Clueless

- Static

- Cold

- Lifeless

- Boring

Never leave your team members out in the cold.

Team members who are not speaking at the moment should be alert and taking notes, no talking amongst themselves, no distractions, no playing with phones or computers.

Everyone should be on the ready and able to jump in and support the mission at any time.

If any team members are not active participants in the presentation, then they shouldn't be there. Silent or bored wallflowers do not advance your cause. Involve them or leave them at home.

Never put on a presentation that you would not want to sit through yourself.

This should be pretty obvious. If you hate it or are bored by it, just imagine what we think.

Project! (emphásis on the second sylláble)

Nope, nothing to do with slide projectors. Not this time.

The Art of Projection is:

> *"The process of intensifying speech and actions so that everyone in the audience can clearly understand."*
>
> *Oakland School for the Arts*

You need to make sure the person farthest away from you can hear and understand and see everything you say and do.

This is not done by shouting or over-emoting but by speaking simple words strongly with clear enunciation at a listenable cadence and comfortable pace.

Of course you're nervous, especially if you haven't practiced enough or committed your outline to memory, but that means you have to be extra careful to not speed up, or mumble, or talk to your shoes or get all jittery.

That person at the back is just as important and they need to clearly hear what you're saying.

Cover all your bases when speaking and address everyone in the group at various points in your presentation. Make the person in the back feel like they are part of the personal conversation with you.

You want everyone to understand what you're saying, right?

Timing & delivery

... are absolutely crucial elements for making your presentation effective and memorable.

You can learn a lot from watching speeches by accomplished public speakers like:

- Barack Obama

- Bill Clinton

- John F. Kennedy

- Margaret Thatcher

- Martin Luther King, Jr.

- Ronald Reagan

- Steve Jobs

- Winston Churchill

And you can also learn a lot by studying great actors and successful comedians.

Also study gestures, pacing, positioning, and how accomplished speakers and presenters use their hands to underscore their words. Your hands are not flippers, nor should they be fidgety appendages. Use them to effectively accentuate your words and your key points.

Nextslideplease, nextslideplease, nextslideplease

If you've built up any rhythm or excitement or tension in your presentation, you deflate it every time you ask for someone to advance the slides while you stand there like a goober and wait.

If at all possible, be in control of your timing and sequencing.

Either carry a tablet with you and operate it directly, or carry a remote clicker discretely in one hand and know how to use it.

Whatever you do, don't be this guy:

Slides going backwards instead of forwards.

Jumping ahead a slide and then jumping back again.

Going too fast, or skipping over slides altogether.

Clicking frantically but nothing happening at all.

If you're that incapable of running a simple slide show, then you shouldn't be using one. *Or working on any of our projects.*

The last thing you want to do in front of a potential client is look unprepared, clumsy and incompetent.

You'd be much better off flapping your arms and jumping about and acting out your slide show instead. Believe it or not, I've seen it done, and to great effect.

You're getting sleepy, very sleepy...

If you think about it, requiring your audience to continuously stare at repetitive slides in a dark room while you drone on in a dull monotone voice is not much different than the technique used to induce hypnosis.

Is that really the effect you want to have?!?

Don't be guilty of *numbing down* your audience!

And if you use Prezi (think "dizzy") you run the risk of giving your audience vertigo. It won't matter what you say if they only remember the motion sickness and nausea.

Interview do's and don't's

- Don't send your "Song and Dance Man."

- Don't send a clueless Principal (unless they are there to show high level commitment and to introduce the PM).

- Don't send your slick Marketing VP. Or your hot office "babe."

- Don't send wallflowers who sit and say nothing.

- Show confidence, not showmanship or arrogance.

- Don't waste our time.

- Don't be boring.

- Don't pander.

- Show brevity and clarity.

- Only one key point per slide.

- Don't dim the room lights.

- Don't use annoying slide transitions, sounds, cutesy graphics.

- Don't hand out copies of the slides.

- Don't make lame attempts at jokes or humor.

- Be genuine.

- Include personal stories if relevant, revealing and short.

- Avoid gratuitous name-dropping, bragging, platitudes.

- Try to anticipate any "gotchas" and "what ifs."

- Tell us about a major surprise and how you dealt with it.

- Tell us why you want this job, why you want to work for us.

- End exactly on time (or 30 seconds before).

- Tell us something fascinating or unusual about each project, and perhaps even about each team member.

- Don't trash talk or talk stink about the competition, or previous clients, or prospective clients, or anyone else for that matter.

- Don't wave reports or previous studies at us.

- Don't bring only graybeards. Let's see some youth and energy along with the wisdom and experience.

- Answer all questions – an "I don't know" is a "no" vote.

- Have a good answer for every question. Even if your CEO just got indicted, tell us about the new procedures you've put in place so it doesn't happen again.

- No clunky samples requiring wasteful setup time.

- Nothing messy.

- Be courteous, knowledgeable, respectful, all the good Boy Scout traits.

- Make us forget the other applicants.

- Be more awesome than everybody else.

- Don't end with a summary – end with a memorable Big Finish.

- Think of the best presentations you've ever attended. What made them great? Now do the same for your presentations.

Surprise us in a good way

Everyone claims to be "leaders and experts in their field" but how do you prove this in your interview?

How about doing something innovative at the interview itself (like the example with three jars of water), or by telling us about something really cool you've done on a project (like using elephants), or some surprising something that happened and how your team saved the day.

Give us something to remember you over all the others.

- Maybe you discovered a unique way to save time or money on a big project?

- Maybe you opted to incorporate an important community concern in your last project?

- Maybe you have some really impressive lessons learned that show your creativity and client-focused awareness?

- Maybe you include community leaders and cultural practitioners where appropriate in your more sensitive projects?

- Maybe you do things that show you're more than just workers on routine projects?

- Maybe you have a unique approach that continually leads to project success?

- Maybe you've worked on the most awesome project ever and came out of it leagues ahead of where you were before?

- Maybe you took a stinker of a project and managed to make everyone end up smelling like roses?

Ever won a project using Feng Shui?

While preparing to interview for an important cemetery project, we learned that the client was a recent convert to the ancient Chinese philosophy known as Feng Shui.

But their interest was far more financial than metaphysical. They found they could charge the Asian community much more for burial sites blessed by a Feng Shui Master and this had resulted in literally millions of dollars in increased sales.

So what did we do? To their complete surprise we brought their favorite Feng Shui Master to the interview as a valued team member – and they greeted him with hugs and kisses!

Did it matter much what we actually said in the interview? Not really. We basically had it won when we walked in the door.

Moral: If it's important to the client, make sure it's important to you too. Even better if it's something really unusual and special. And even more so if it makes them lots of money.

What could possibly go wrong?

- Can't find the room or the building

- Projector doesn't work

- Pointer doesn't work

- Computer problems

- Wrong presentation

- Fonts not embedded

- Late start

- Room too big, room too small

- Room too hot, room too cold

- Less time than anticipated

- Team member is a no-show

- Room too bright

- Lights won't dim

- Lights too dim

- Stage fright

- Nervousness

- Talking too fast

- Awkward postures and gestures

- Out of time

- Interview board asks unplanned-for questions

- No questions at all from the board. Either you totally blew it/nailed it or they've already made their selection.

There can be power in having no power

Years ago I was in a traditional British folk music band performing on stage at a festival concert hall when halfway through the set all the electrical power on the stage suddenly went out. No microphones, no amplifiers.

After a second or two of shared quizzical looks, one of the members shouted "to the stands!" We jumped off the stage, ran halfway up the steps in the seating area and then, with our backs to each other launched into a series of acapella songs to a very surprised and subsequently very enthusiastic and very supportive audience.

When we needed a musical instrument one of us would make a big deal of madly dashing back to the stage to get it while one of the others shouted out the introduction to the next song.

People outside the hall heard music, saw an empty stage, but ended up pouring into the venue in droves to see what all the excitement was about.

Something like this could conceivably happen during your presentation – loss of microphone, PowerPoint problems, computer issues, projector bulb burns out, you name it. Be ready, prepare for the unexpected.

Always have a Plan B (or be able to come up with one at a moment's notice). If you do, it will tell us a lot more about you than you realize.

The problems with handouts

1. If handed out before the presentation, the Selection Committee will get ahead of you.

2. If handed out during the presentation the Selection Committee may get lost.

3. If handed out after the presentation the Selection Committee may forget what you presented.

4. If handed out at all, they'll very likely get tossed since we already have your written proposal and the interview is all about your personal presentation.

Interview Q's

Here are some sample questions that could easily pop up during the Q&A portion of your Selection Committee interview:

- Have you done this type of project before?

- How is our project similar to one you've done?

- Tell us about a design challenge and how you fixed it.

- What is your definition of good design?

- Tell us about an innovative approach you've used.

- Any anticipated challenges or issues with this project?

- What else has your team done together?

- How do you manage unforeseen problems?

- How do you manage subconsultants and deliverables?

- How do you accelerate a schedule?

- How do you manage the budget?

- Describe your QA/QC process in detail.

- How do you handle errors and omissions?

- What are two key lessons you learned from your last project?

- Have you worked with us before? When and where?

- Are you familiar with the site?

- Tell us about your capacity and current workload.

- How do you communicate and share information?

- What added value will your team bring to the project?

- Why would you like to win this project?

- Why should we pick you?

- What questions do you have for us?

Wrong answer

The shortlist interview was for a large military aviation project in Colorado and the architectural firm I worked for was a subconsultant to a large nationwide firm who was the prime.

During the Q&A session at the end of the interview they asked the larger firm's Project Manager how much time would he be spending on the project if selected.

His answer? "10-15%."

Gasp.

Confronted in the hallway afterwards by the other team members, he cluelessly replied "Do you think that was too much?"

Needless to say, they weren't selected.

Turn the tables

What if you were us?

Would you hire you?

Put yourself in our place and see your efforts in a completely different (and far more realistic) light.

Don't just do a standard proofread of your proposal, and don't just mumble through a half-hearted rehearsal. Do a full-blown mock interview. Be brutal. Be relentless. No holds barred.

Get your toughest, meanest, most sarcastic employee to mimic a Selection Committee. Or impose upon an impartial third party. Do it anonymously if you need to.

Voluntarily feed yourself to the sharks, throw yourself in the lion's den, or use whatever metaphor you need to that gets you to the gates of hell in front of the firing squad.

Use a scorecard, follow the RFP, ask pointy questions.

Show no mercy.

For this exercise, proving yourself is far more important than mere proofreading. This is a full-out test of your training and your mettle.

Such a self-inflicted trial by fire might be just the wake-up call you need.

With luck, the actual interview will be a breeze by comparison, and your battle-tested veterans will now be able to handle anything the Selection Committee might throw at you.

Video pitfalls and pratfalls

If your interview is conducted by video conference there are a host of issues to consider to make sure you don't look like some highway-blinded deer or awkward amateur YouTube zombie.

Video conferencing is typically conducted in one of two ways:

1. Group setting – everyone in your group in one room together with a single webcam, with a similar setup for the interview committee.

2. Individual setting – everyone on their own personal computer appearing in little boxes on the screen like *Hollywood Squares* or the opening sequence of *The Brady Bunch* TV show.

Either way, the same basic principles apply:

-   Long before you log in, make sure everything works. The webcam, the microphone, the sound, the lighting, the setting. Everything.

-   Position your webcam as close to the video display as possible, preferably near the top center and not off to the side or down on a desk or table somewhere.

-   For a group setting, invest in a high quality video system with high resolution that can pan and zoom and incorporate images and documents.

-   For an individual setting, make sure each person has a webcam with high quality video and microphone, or perhaps a headset with integral microphone. Make sure they are in a quiet workspace and won't distract others or be distracted by others.

-   Conversation timing and staging is way different for video communicating and visual space is limited. Know who's talking when and what's on or off screen.

- Speak distinctly and clearly, no shouting. Allow for any lag in the audio signal and avoid interrupting or multiple people talking at once.

- Check what's behind you. Make sure your background is professional with no distractions, no people walking by, no photobombs. How many YouTube videos have you seen with someone's underwear all over the bed in the background? 'Nuff said.

- Know when the video camera and microphone are on and when they are off. How many politicians have been tripped up with inappropriate comments because they didn't think the microphone was still on? Be very careful what you say until you are sure the system is totally off.

- If you are not speaking for an extended period of time. mute the microphone to minimize echo or interference, but make sure it's on before you start speaking.

- For both group and individual settings, do not engage in any non-interview activities like checking email, reading, texting, taking phone calls or talking privately to anyone in the room or off camera. You need to be focused and fully present at all times.

- Don't rustle papers unnecessarily or tap the table or the microphone. Turn off notifications on your cellphone.

- Dress appropriately for the camera. Dress for contrast with your surroundings, but bright white, wild patterns, stripes and polka dots can create screen disturbances.

- Remember – everything you say can be heard by everyone on the other side and everything you do is visible on screen to the other party. And who knows, they might even be recording it. So no unintentional funny faces and no fidgeting or picking your nose. Be natural and professional at all times.

Best interview advice ever

"Be brief, be brilliant, be gone."

Hubert J. Carter, Jr., Deputy for Small Business,
US Army Corps of Engineers, Omaha District

SELECTION SECRETS

Now that you've made it through some basic thoughts about submittals and interviews, here are things that can go on behind the scenes that you need to be aware of...

SECRET #1

It's all about us, not you.

Huh? Think that doesn't make any sense? Think again.

It's not about how great and wonderful you are...

...it's about our problem/need and who can best fix it for us.

- Focus on our needs, not yours.
- Show us you understand us and our business.
- Show us how you'd fix our problem.
- Show us you've done this successfully for others.

Write for us, not for you.

- Be mindful of who your audience is.
- Speak our language.
- Cut irrelevant material.
- Make it easy for us to read and review.
- Get to the point.

SECRET #2

The RFP doesn't always tell the whole story.

Would it surprise you to know that RFP's are sometimes slapped together fairly quickly, with whole sections sometimes cut-and-pasted from previous solicitations?

It happens. People are busy, they grab what's available, and the person writing the solicitation might not even be from the end-user customer or department.

So it's important that you know the *why* of the RFP so your proposal can more directly address the problem.

If the RFP is your first knowledge of the project, then you're already behind the 8-ball.

You should try to meet with the client or agency way ahead of the RFP hitting the street. You should know well in advance what they need, what projects are coming up, how the acquisition process works, how the funding mechanisms work, etc.

You also need to be able to read between the lines to find out what the client really wants or needs.

If you can do this, then you can write a proposal that you know will address our needs regardless of the language in the RFP.

It's much better to hit the proposal target with a focused rifle shot than with a poorly aimed shotgun blast.

A little cultural awareness can go a long way

Many years ago there was an RFP and design competition to build a new airport terminal in Central America.

Of course, all the North American firms trotted out their standard terminal designs and details.

Except for one.

They were the lone firm to include a large covered public gathering space as part of their design and they were instantly selected as the winner.

The reason? They were the only firm that knew that air travel for a family member in that country was a pretty big social event, with the entire extended family showing up hours before the flight to eat, drink and party and wish the traveler well.

The RFP never mentioned such a space.

But they'd been there and they knew it was important to include.

SECRET #3

We're desperate to cull the herd.

Keep in mind we're looking for *The One* out of a potentially huge list of contenders.

Instead of intently poring over every page of every submittal, we need to get the pile down to a more manageable size as quickly as possible.

You've heard the term *non-responsive*? That's our friend.

Not follow explicit instructions?	Toss.
Leave something out?	Toss.
Forget to answer a key question?	Toss.
Submit late?	Toss.
Forget to sign a key document?	Toss.

And this is just for the first cut. Know there are many other factors that can also land your well-wrought efforts in the rubbish heap.

For want of a letter, a proposal was lost

Everything looked good – the team was strong, the proposal was well written, and it was submitted early.

Fifteen minutes before the cutoff time I got a call from the university selection committee telling me that everything was fine but the appendix was missing a signed letter from the president of the only out-of-state firm on the team.

The letter just needed to state that the firm would become registered to do business in the state if selected.

From a principal, out-of-state, signed, 15 minutes before the bell.

The proposal coordinator had missed this one tiny detail.

There was no way to come up with such a letter in 15 minutes.

They threw all 16 copies in the trash.

SECRET #4

We've heard it all before.

All of it.

   "We are leaders in blah blah blah…"

   "We have state-of-the-art blah blah blah…"

   "We have extensive experience in blah blah blah…"

   "We have a proprietary QA/QC process blah blah blah…"

Here's another acronym for you:

SSDD

(same sh*t different day)

Surprise us. Please.

Get our attention.

Be awesome.

Wow us.

Tell us something we don't know, about a problem we didn't know we had, and why you're the perfect team to solve it on time and on budget.

SECRET #5

Most submittals are reviewed in a matter of minutes.

Assuming your submittal has made the first cut that checks for completeness and responsiveness it will then go into the stack to be reviewed by the Selection Committee.

You have no idea how quickly proposals are reviewed.

Although some submittals are broken apart and passed out to the various committee members, most of the time they are reviewed by all members while sitting around a large table.

IF you're lucky, we'll spend maybe 5 seconds on each page.

Yes, 5 seconds/page.

DO THE MATH:

5 second review per page

x 100 pages

x 25 submittals

_____

= 3.5 hours without a break

So, maybe 5-10 minutes per proposal is all the time you'll get.

SECRET #6

We don't read your every word.

Do you really think we carefully read every single one of your exquisitely crafted sentences and paragraphs, page after page?

Fat chance of that ever happening. No time.

When we initially sit down with our pile of submittals we will typically start with a quick flip-through to see who you are and if you've covered the main points in the RFP.

It goes something like this:

- A quick glance at the org chart to see who's on the team.

- A quick flip through the résumés to see who's who and if they're qualified.

- A quick look at the projects to see if they're relevant.

- A quick glance at the Project Understanding to see if you really do understand it.

- A quick check for generic bs versus custom responses.

- A quick search for that special something that puts you head and shoulders above the pack.

SECRET #7

Some of us never read your cover letter.

How many of you spend hours wordsmithing the perfect cover letter?

How many of you just cobble something together? Or treat it like a generic Letter of Transmittal?

Either way, chances are fairly slim that any reviewer will actually read it.

Especially if it starts off with standard clichés or general bs like:

- "We are pleased to submit…"

- "Attached herewith for the aforementioned…"

- "We are leaders in blah blah blah…"

If it doesn't look like it is worth reading, we won't read it.

If it's over one page, we probably won't read it.

If it has tiny margins and a sea of incomprehensible text, I can guarantee you that no one will touch it. In fact, something like that does far more harm than good.

SECRET #8

The Executive Summary might be the only thing we read.

Time is short, and in theory the Executive Summary should be a concise condensation of everything in your proposal.

If it looks like you *get it* then you might very well get the project. Or advance to the shortlist interview.

If your Executive Summary rambles or misses the point, then the reviewer might toss it right then and there and not waste any more time slogging through your whole submittal.

It's been reported that Winston Churchill would not read any briefing papers longer than one page. What if you had only one page for your entire proposal – could you do it? That's the Executive Summary.

SECRET #9

We might not even open your SOQ.

True, it's happened.

And it can be for good or bad reasons.

If we know you, your team, your workload, your capabilities – you might just be a shoe-in.

Conversely, there are times when the committee members know that certain firms are way out of their league, are total unknowns, or there might even be political reasons for exclusion.

Yep. Set aside, unopened.

Remember that bit about needing to cull the herd?

Either way, it can make for a nice quick selection process.

No need to read

One of my first municipal Selection Committee meetings was called to pick a firm for a large water tower project.

The members already knew the relative qualifications of all the firms who submitted.

So we discussed the merits of each firm at length while the SOQ's sat unopened on the table the entire time.

We also talked about what other city projects the firms were currently working on, workload, etc.

And then we came up with a unanimous decision.

Never touched the books.

SECRET #10

If you follow our criteria clearly and in order it will make our jobs a lot easier.

I know, I know, you want to tell your story in your own unique way.

Or you're lazy and just want to submit the same old tired boilerplate language.

But if we're using a scorecard based on the RFP criteria, and you follow that format exactly, then it makes it a lot easier for us to review and check.

There's usually plenty of room elsewhere to tell your story and to wow us with your wonderfulness. Which we might actually read if it looks interesting and if you've made our review easy so far.

SECRET #11

We don't want the kitchen sink.

Why do so many firms think they have to throw everything into their proposal whether it is pertinent or not?

Throwing everything you've ever done into a huge pile and then dumping it on the selection committee in hopes that maybe something in that morass will stick simply does not work.

Irrelevant information, gratuitous filler and miscellaneous extraneous crap work against you.

Don't be guilty of committing Information Overdose.

Read your own proposal from cover to cover — is it something you or anyone else would want to read or look at in any depth?

Does it tell your story effectively?

Does it answer the RFP's questions and address the client's needs?

You might think you're just giving us everything including the kitchen sink, but we'll wish you also included the toilet so we could flush it all down the drain.

You waste our time and we'll reciprocate by ensuring you've wasted yours.

SECRET #12

We like short answers.

Yes.

If you can answer any of our questions with a single word, do it.

Long rambling sentences and paragraphs will only demonstrate your inability to think clearly.

Short, sweet and to the point wins every day.

BLUF or Fluff?

In military parlance "BLUF" means "<u>B</u>ottom <u>L</u>ine <u>U</u>p <u>F</u>ront."

Don't beat around the bush, don't hide your key information in a mountain of unreadable text. Get to the point. Fast.

And irrelevant extraneous fluff? Don't even go there.

More is not necessarily better. More is just… more.

SECRET #13

We might be totally unfamiliar with the project.

Selection committees can be drawn from a wide variety of client or governmental departments, some of whom may be only marginally familiar with the type of work involved or the firms who have submitted.

With luck, some members will be knowledgeable about the needs of the project, and are perhaps the very people who got the project and the funding approved through their own internal version of a selection committee.

Other members might be from a purchasing department, or maybe a department head is sitting in for another department head, or perhaps an appointed or elected official or two might be present.

SECRET #14

We're not all technical experts.
(don't assume we know the acronyms and jargon)

A typical Selection Committee could consist of:

- Contracting Officer
- Purchasing Officer
- Chief Engineer
- Vice President of Planning
- Project Customer
- Commander/Department Head
- Small Business Deputy
- Attorney
- City Council member
- Football coach
- Alumni Representative
- University President
- Architect
- Facility Manager
- Director of Construction Services
- Chief Maintenance Officer

SECRET #15

We're all looking for different things.

Depending on individual backgrounds, interests, biases and pet peeves, each of us on the Selection Committee will likely focus on different portions of your submittal.

The contracting officers and management types will be most interested in your project controls and fiscal responsibility.

The engineers will be looking closely at your technical abilities.

The end-user will be studying your Project Understanding and Project Approach.

The client's PM will be scrutinizing the team's PM and team's résumés.

The Small Business Liaison will care most about the extent of your Small Business and DBE participation.

So, write with everyone in mind.

Cover all the bases by addressing all the individual concerns.

Make sure there is something for everybody. If they don't see what they're looking for it will count against you.

SECRET #16

Committee members often have favorites.

If certain firms have a reputation for performing exceedingly well, of course they will be favorites.

Even if you're not the most qualified we might give you the project anyway because we enjoy working with you and have a high enough confidence in your abilities to get the job done.

Or maybe a committee member worked for one of the firms previously and had a good experience.

In some instances it might be because somebody just likes someone in one of the submitting firms, or is related to them.

There's not much you can do about this, except to work toward becoming a future favorite.

SECRET #17

Sometimes we already know who we want.
(and the RFP is just a formality)

A follow-up to the favorites secret...

Most government agencies are required to publicly solicit RFP's even if they know who they want. They typically need to get at least three proposals.

Sometimes it's a done deal, a mere formality, a pretense of public participation.

And sometimes it's a *Hail Mary* just to see if anyone else out there might turn up.

So if you hear of a proposal where they're only asking for three submittals, be wary. Unless you're fairly certain you have the "in" you're probably just feeding their wastebasket.

SECRET #18

Don't assume we know anything about you.
(but we might know more than you think)

In theory, every submittal is a standalone document and all are treated equally and blindly. Right.

In reality, we probably know something about you already, either through the grapevine or through personal experience.

This can be good or bad, depending.

Will it color our selection? Probably.

But you need to present your qualifications assuming that the paper in front of us is all we have to go by. If we already know you, it provides written reinforcement and confirmation.

SECRET #19

If we don't know you, you are facing an uphill climb.

Think about it. If there are two proposals with essentially equal qualifications and we know one of the firms but not the other, who are we going to pick?

We get proposals from out of the blue all the time and often shake our heads wondering why.

- Why are they submitting?
- Who are these guys?
- Why haven't they come and talked to us beforehand?

Conversely, if we do know you and you've screwed up really bad somewhere along the way – similar uphill climb.

Out of the blue, into the black

In addition to the submittals from the usual suspects for a particular CIP project, there was a new one from a firm I'd never heard of.

I looked at the cover and it was pretty homemade, so that made me think they were a fairly low-budget operation.

I looked at the org chart but didn't recognize any of the firms.

I looked at the résumés but didn't know any of the people.

I looked at the projects and none of them jumped out and grabbed my attention.

Pass.

Now if they'd come by my office a week or two before and introduced themselves and given me a capability briefing I would have looked at their submittal with very different eyes instead of casting it into the dark.

SECRET #20

We can't embarrass ourselves or our superiors
by betting on a complete unknown.

Project execution and success are crucially important on the
client side, even more so than for the submitting firm.

Political careers have been won and lost over failed projects, as
have government careers all up and down the chain of
command.

Put yourself in our shoes – would you hire someone you knew
nothing about to design or manage your multi-million dollar
project?

But that doesn't mean a new firm can't break into the market, it
just makes it a lot more difficult.

We don't want our project to be a first-time learning experience
for either of us, or something that just keeps your employees
busy. Or something that could potentially go down in flames.

Little project, big project

A water utility agency I worked for needed an engineering firm to design a simple concrete foundation for a new bolted-steel water tank.

About this same time there was a firm who had been coming by on a regular basis inquiring about upcoming projects and offering their services whenever needed. They made a point of letting the agency know they wanted to earn their business.

We selected this firm for the tank foundation project although they'd not previously worked with us, but thinking this would be a good test of their abilities. The project was really small but it went really well.

Based on this successful previous project and ongoing client relationship, this same firm was subsequently selected to design and manage a large $4M water line project.

SECRET #21

Different selection committees make different choices.

Believe it or not, we're all human. Different people look for different things and will rate various criteria differently.

Sometimes a previous selection is nullified for a variety of reasons and a new committee is called. There's no guarantee that the number one firm in the first go around will be the winner the second time.

It's a new day with a new dealer and the cards are reshuffled.

SECRET #22

Sometimes it's just not your turn.

Not true so much for large government agencies, but quite often the case for smaller towns and municipalities.

There can sometimes be a sense of needing to spread the work around.

Sometimes this is politically motivated, sometimes not.

If so, there's nothing in your qualifications that will change that fact.

Accept it graciously and work to ensure the next opportunity comes your way.

SECRET #23

We might have a different project in mind for you.

Don't jump up and down and complain because you didn't get selected for such and such project.

The committee might know about other projects coming up that would be a perfect fit for your firm.

Don't ruin that chance with any sour grapes or unprofessional whining.

SECRET #24

It might have nothing to do with your submittal or your qualifications.

This is a tough one. In some situations there can be a host of outside forces and extenuating circumstances that will affect the selection committee process.

You might have the most brilliant qualifications in the world, but any one of these things could trip you up:

- One of your team members is notoriously difficult to work with (PM, Principal, sub, etc.).

- You really messed up _____ project.

- Your accounting system is a pain to work with.

- Your plans require too many revisions and too many RFI's.

- The Mayor/City Council/Governor/Contracting Officer is mad at you about _____.

- You don't respond quickly enough to phone calls or emails (slow or unresponsive).

- You plans, specs and reports are poorly written, with lots of typos and mistakes.

- You consistently over-promise and under-deliver.

- You are from a different town/region and the preference is to support local firms.

- You are a branch office of a national firm and the preference is to support local firms.

- You can't keep a schedule and consistently miss deadlines.

- You can't design to budget.

- You have a bad reputation in the community.

- You are too busy.

- You always try to gouge the fee.

- You are known for bait and switch.

- You don't present well at public meetings.

- You are dishonest, argumentative, etc.

- You never contact client staff.

- You are rude to client staff.

- You pester client staff too much during projects.

- You have high staff turnover.

- You are not financially stable.

- Your company's partners do not get along.

- You are parties to lawsuits.

- You file lawsuits.

- You protest selections.

- You have language and translation difficulties.

- You outsource your production.

- Nepotism, family ties, problems with exes, neighborhood disputes, etc.

- Some reviewers can be guilty of racism, prejudice.

- Some reviewers can be biased (Army vs Navy, OU vs UT)

- Your firm is a total unknown – a mystery firm.

- You have no track record.

- You are too big for the job.

- You are too small for the job.

- You have antiquated technology.

- You are known for Armchair Engineering.

- You partake in excessive schmoozing and politicking.

- You support questionable activities ("Vote No" on bond issues, etc.)

- You allow inappropriate employee behavior.

- You've bad-mouthed the client or the agency in print or in public.

- Maybe somebody has an ax to grind.

- Or maybe someone owes somebody else a favor.

- Perhaps you or a team member has a black eye from a previous project or teaming relationship.

- Maybe there's some "home-cookin' goin' on" in favor of a particular local firm.

- _____

- _____

- _____

- _____

Caught with hand in cookie jar?

When I was a City Engineer there was an engineering firm that tried to substantially over-bill for a large infrastructure analysis project.

Was their internal accounting so bad that they inadvertently invoiced for more than the contract amount? Even though they were far from finished?

Or did they think they could get away with it and we'd just pay it anyway?

Either way, you can probably imagine how this pretty much ruined their chances for any future considerations.

SECRET #25

Location, Location, Location.

Do you have any experience working in the same geographical location as the project?

Do you have any clue where the project is located?

If we need a quick response, how far away is your Project Manager and your team from us?

How far are you and your team from the project location?

We're also concerned about multiple branch office and team member locations and how you communicate, coordinate and prioritize things long distance.

Working on my project? Or not.

A subconsultant in a remote branch office was on the verge of missing a key deadline for a large military project I was working on, and they seemed oblivious to repeated emails and phone messages inquiring about the status of submitting plans to be reviewed.

What to do? I called and told them I would be arriving at their office the following Monday and Tuesday so we could sit down and do an onboard over-the-shoulder review to simplify and speed up the design process.

Well, they said, "he's been busy this week, and he's in a meeting on Monday and he's not available on Tuesday."

To which I replied, "so... you just told me that he's not working on my project."

Funny, a set of plans miraculously arrived over the weekend.

SECRET #26

Size does matter.

- Is your company too small for this project?

- Is your company too big for this project?

- What about your upcoming workload?

- What kind of depth do you have in your bench?

We're concerned about competing priorities and want to make sure you can handle our projects.

SECRET #27

Bribes, favors, advertising tchotchkes, tasty treats – all a big no-no.

Of course we'd love a Krispy Kreme doughnut, or a fancy pen, or even a hot cup of coffee or something stronger (like a really stiff drink). But no can do.

Don't hand out your business cards either – it wastes our time and yours to give them to each committee member. We've already got your contact info and we're not going to save your card for later. Same for your team members' cards. Don't.

And don't dump a bunch of useless company brochures or other materials on us either. I promise you they will go straight to the circular file as soon as you walk out the door.

SECRET #28

We can easily see through your bs.

Why do so many firms fill their proposals and presentations with huge heaping piles of bs, unsubstantiated claims, outrageous exaggerations and even outright fabrications?

Do they really think we're stupid enough to fall for any of it?

We can spot it a mile away.

And we've heard it all a million times before.

In addition to telling us you're borderline dishonest, it also tells us you haven't a clue what you're talking about.

Why would we hire someone like that?

SECRET #29

If your proposal looks crappy we'll assume the rest of your work is too.

Your proposal is a work product, just as much as your plans, specifications and reports. If it's pretty much junk, we don't want to imagine what your other work is like.

I know, I know, it's not YOUR work – it's from your Marketing Department, or Publications Department, or your poor undertrained and underpaid admins and interns, etc.

Wrong.

It's still your work. Same company.

You're tarred with the same brush whether you like it or not.

A poorly organized or poorly prepared proposal is a direct reflection of your corporate quality.

And if your submittal is loaded with typos and mistakes? If there's no overarching reason to select you, you're toast.

SECRET #30

We hate "The Cram."

You know what I'm talking about.

- tiny fonts

- tiny margins

- no spaces

- no white space

- shoveling in as much crap per page as possible

Don't think you're being clever and gaming the system by trying to beat the page count. Or just trying to include way too much information by squeezing in everything you possibly can.

There's a good reason why we often specify the font and the point size – to prevent this sort of nonsense from happening.

This is a test – can you tell your story in the space allotted? And is it readable?

Make it fit, not by cramming but through skillful writing.

Don't risk really pissing us off.

I can guarantee you if it's not readable, we won't read it.

SECRET #31

Sometimes we're told who to pick by higher-ups. (but it doesn't happen as much as it used to)

Politics? Favoritism? Bias? Discrimination?

Although we often hire who we like and trust as long as their qualifications are close enough, the Big Boss may weigh in sometimes.

If so, there's precious little we can do about it other than to say "yes, sir" or "yes, ma'am."

We don't want to lose our jobs by defying orders or displeasing our boss.

And we'll make it look like it was a fair selection.

Luckily, this is getting rarer and rarer but unfortunately can still happen.

What can you do about it? Absolutely nothing.

SECRET #32

We might just be fishing.

This falls in the category of dirty pool and unsportsmanlike conduct, but it can happen on rare occasions.

Potential warning signs:

- "Project has not been authorized"
- "Funds have not been allocated"
- "TBD"

We might have a need and a CIP schedule, but we might be using the submittal process to refine the scope or the budget.

That's called "partnering" right? But at your expense.

Or maybe we're hoping for a last minute budget adjustment, congressional add or end-of-year "tails money" funding.

Just be aware before you start counting your chickens.

From a recent Dilbert comic strip by Scott Adams:

INTERVIEWER
Tell me your process for solving this sort of problem.

INTERVIEWEE
I would hold fake job interviews and ask people how to solve it.

SECRET #33

We don't care what projects your company completed 20 years ago.

Sorry, but we're not huge fans of ancient history. You might really care about your company history, but we don't.

"Since 1938, etc." means what to us? Don't get caught up in your own mythology.

All those folks are probably long dead and gone by now.

All we care about is what you can do today.

If the projects are too old, it's doubtful the people who worked on them are still with the company.

Or maybe you purchased this experience when you acquired another company?

Staff experience plays much better than corporate experience.

A long history of involvement in a particular field or type of project can indicate you're either resting on your laurels or you're really the go-to experienced experts. It's up to you to make sure we know which one it is.

But we're far more interested in the experience of the staff you're proposing for our project, not generalized corporate history or warm fuzzy memoirs.

SECRET #34

Community involvement can be a big plus.

Not so much for state or federal projects, but for local boards and municipalities it can make a difference if a firm supports local causes and is working hard to make a positive difference in the community.

All of these can boost your company image:

- Sponsorships

- Gratis labor

- Community leadership

- Professional society leadership

- Non-profit board memberships

- Non-profit donations

- Community projects

SECRET #35

Interview Committee members might be different than the proposal Selection Committee.

Don't assume the interview is just a continuation of the conversation you started with your paper submittal.

The Interview Committee members have probably already read through your proposal.

If so, they've very likely read it in more detail than the initial Selection Committee.

Be ready for questions about anything and everything in your submittals. If you weren't intimately involved in the writing and preparation of your proposal you'll need to know all of it inside and out.

And be especially ready for any questions that might arise from any reading between the lines – those will usually be the trickiest to answer. But depending on how you handle it, it can be an opportunity to dramatically showcase your expertise and abilities.

SECRET #36

The interview is not about your qualifications.

"WHAT?!?"

That's right. We've got your paper submittal to tell us about your qualifications, so there's no need to rehash all that.

The interview is all about *who* and *how* and not the *what*.

I've heard numerous clients and Selection Committee members say:

"Let us know who you are"

We want to know how you think and how you approach your work and how you'd solve our immediate needs.

We want to know how your team will ensure project success.

We want to know how your Project Manager will drive the schedule and the deliverables and manage costs.

We want to know who is going to do what and why and how.

We want you to show us you can handle whatever our project might throw at you.

If you've made it to the interview, then we're ok with your quals. Now is our chance to check the team for fit.

SECRET #37

We can tell from the interview if your team plays well together.

Believe it or not, we can tell if you're just throwing bodies at the project or if you're giving us an experienced team.

If your other team members just sit there, bored, that's a big red flag.

If you can't remember a team member's name, that's a huge red flag.

If you can't give us good examples of successful projects you've worked on together, we'll assume you have no idea if you can work together well or not.

SECRET #38

We can learn a lot from your demeanor and interactions before and after the interview.

Do you think we only pay attention to you once the clock starts? Think again! How you handle yourself, your equipment, your team – we see it all.

Chances are you may not have met or seen any of us before, so be careful from the moment you leave your office or home town. Sometimes we bring in reviewers from out of town, and they might even be on the same flight.

If you were drunk on your ass at the hotel bar the night before, or made inappropriate passes at the woman sitting next to you, we might have seen it if we were there too. And what if that woman is now sitting in front of you as a member of the Selection Committee?

If you take forever trying to get your computer to boot or projector to work, we'll see you as unprepared for something as simple as that and doubt your ability to run a real project.

If you suddenly go into a fake *show business* mode when the interview starts, we'll really question your professionalism and sincerity. We don't want an act, we want you to be you.

And if you take forever to break down your equipment and gear afterwards, cutting into the next team's time, that's a pretty bad final impression.

Make sure you've got your act together from start to finish.

SECRET #39

Attention to detail is important. Every detail. From what you say to what you write to how you look.

Remember, we're looking for ways to cull the herd, to quickly weed out the bad ones so we can concentrate on the top firms.

Spell our names accurately, pronounce them correctly, know your stuff and give us error-free submittals and presentations.

Be ready for tough questions during the Q&A portion of the interview or during the interview itself. If you come across as not knowing the answers or the details, you might as well go home.

"The devil is in the details."

Ludwig Mies van der Rohe

SECRET #40

Appearances are important.

It's always a nice surprise to see someone actually pay special attention to how they look and present themselves to the client and to the interview as opposed to just *suiting up*.

You always want to dress slightly better than the interview board, but not so much that it's a noticeable distinction.

If you're in the Deep South, a double-breasted suit and vest will instantly brand you as an outsider. If you look like a Damn Yankee from up north, that for sure ain't gonna cut it with any good ol' Southern boys.

If you're in Hawaii, you need to wear an Aloha shirt to the interview. Seriously. Not ones with naked hula dancers and tropical drinks, but professionally tailored tropical prints by clothiers such as Reyn Spooner or Tori Richard will show a much appreciated understanding of the local culture. Local plays much better than mainlander every time.

But most importantly you need to be comfortable with whatever you're wearing. If this is the first time you've worn a suit or tie in years, your discomfort could be overtly noticeable. Same for women with high heels or plunging necklines.

Dress well, be comfortable, be professional. Nothing garish, nothing inappropriate. No crappy equipment or ratty materials either.

Now if you choose to subtly wear a tie or scarf that just happens to incorporate the client's colors... clever you!

SECRET #41

Protest at your peril.

Yeah, yeah, yeah, so you feel like you should've won instead of the other guy?

Is winning the battle worth losing the war?

You need to always remember that it's our ball and our game.

We set the rules, we enforce them, and if you don't like it that's just tough.

When it comes to SOQ's we can even control which firms are in the initial selection pool.

We don't like working with sore losers.

And you probably don't want to become a pariah.

So suck it up and play nice. Even if it hurts.

Only protest if something is so egregious it would fit nicely on the 6 o'clock news, or if the Supreme Court would rule in your favor.

Company Non Grata

At the end of my first municipal selection committee meeting I noticed the absence of a Statement of Qualifications from a prominent local firm.

A simple question, "What about XYZ Engineering?" was met with deathly silence. Oops.

Turns out they had protested a previous selection. Vigorously.

The company president stormed down to the city offices, demanded to see the scorecards and loudly threatened to go straight to the mayor and city council and maybe even the State Supreme Court.

Wow.

Did anyone in the room want to ever work with a company who acted like that?

Nope.

I never saw their SOQ in any subsequent selection meetings. And when they submitted on individual projects their RFP's remained untouched.

I wonder if they ever realized why they never got any city work?!?

SECRET #42

We're happy to do debriefs.

If you're not selected, most contracting officers will indulge a humble request for a quick debrief.

If you care at all about the client and your proposal – do it.

It's totally free, and you'll learn a lot.

We can't tell you anything about the other firms. But we can tell you how you were scored overall on various criteria.

Be courteous, gracious and ask good questions showing your sincere interest in learning how to do better next time.

This isn't the time to argue or whine. It's over. They selected someone else. Just take your lumps and learn how you can be more effective next time.

Be nice. Be professional. The person on the other end of the phone might be on the next Selection Committee.

Debriefs can also be a good relationship builder since you get to have a one-on-one conversation with the client about your qualifications and how you can present better.

With luck, they'll remember you favorably the next time you call and when your next submittal is sitting in front of them.

HOW TO GET IT RIGHT
(NEXT TIME & EVERY TIME)

- Know us and our business

- Understand our needs

- Understand our timing and financing

- Understand the RFP/acquisition process

- Understand all aspects of the project

- Show us what you excel at

- Match your skills and experience to the RFP

- Bring a strong team

- Write clearly, concisely and convincingly

- Present strong, hit key issues

- Emphasize your track record

- Show how you would solve our problem

- Present with passion

- Provide exceptional value

- Gain our confidence and trust

- Make us forget the other applicants

- Show how you're the perfect partner

- Be more than competent – be exemplary

- Make us want to select you

RESONATE

Make us want or need the services you offer.

DIFFERENTIATE

Show us why you are the best option.

SUBSTANTIATE

Prove yourself and gain our trust.

Based on Mike Schultz's *10 Commandments for Building a Value Proposition that Sells.*

FINAL SECRET

We really do want you to be successful.

We issue lots of RFP's and calls for SOQ's and we need a large pool of qualified firms to choose from to ensure project success.

We want you to do better and we want to make sure what you're submitting to us is the best you can do to accurately describe your capabilities.

If you're successful, we're successful. Everybody wins.

We want you coming to the table qualified and prepared to give us your very best from initial proposal to completed project.

We may not let on, but we want you to knock it out of the park.

If you do good work, are a pleasure to work with, and exceed expectations, we will eagerly welcome your next submittal.

Don't let these Selection Committee secrets remain secrets any longer...

...up your game and win!

Trust

Value

Performance

RESOURCES

Duarte, Nancy. *Slide:ology*. Sebastopol: O'Reilly Media, Inc., 2008.

Duarte, Nancy. *Resonate.* Hoboken: John Wiley & Sons, Inc., 2010.

Duarte, Nancy. *HBR Guide to Persuasive Presentations*. Boston: Harvard Business Review Press, 2012.

Garner, Bryan A. *HBR Guide to Better Business Writing.* Boston: Harvard Business Review Press, 2012.

Godin, Seth. *Whatcha Gonna Do with that Duck?* New York: The Penguin Group, 2012.

Handal, Matt. *Proposal Development Secrets*. West Chester: Matt Handal, 2012.

Kapterev, Alexei. *Presentation Secrets*. Indianapolis: John Wiley & Sons, Inc., 2011.

Karia, Akash. *How to Design TED Worthy Presentation Slides.* Tanzania: CreateSpace, 2015.

Pink, Daniel. *To Sell is Human*. New York: Riverhead Books, 2012.

Port, Michael. *Steal the Show*. Boston: Houghton Mifflin Harcourt, 2015.

Reynolds, Garr. *Presentation Zen*. Berkeley: New Riders, 2012.

Searcy, Tom. *RFPs Suck!* New York: Channel V Books, 2009.

Schultz, Mike and Doerr, John E. *Rainmaking Conversations: Influence, Persuade and Sell in any Situation*. Hoboken: John Wiley & Sons, Inc., 2011.

Trottier, David. *The Screenwriters Bible*. Los Angeles: Silman-James Press, 2014.

US Army Corps of Engineers. *Architect-Engineer Contracting in USACE*. Pamphlet EP 715-1-7, 2012.

US Army Corps of Engineers. *Army Source Selection Manual*. AFARRS, Appendix AA, 2009.

White, Richard. Rolling the Dice in DC. Ketchum: Wood River Technologies, Inc., 2006.

Williams, Robin. *The Non-Designer's Design Book.* Berkeley: Peachpit Press, 2008.

THE AUTHOR

Gary R. Coover

Gary is a licensed professional engineer and principal with Coover Consultants, PLLC, a management and engineering consultancy located in Honolulu, HI and Fayetteville, AR. He has served on countless private and governmental selection committees and has experienced / suffered through seemingly interminable piles of submittals and sometimes excruciating presentations. And some very good ones, too. Thankfully.

He is a former City Engineer who has also worked for large state and county special governmental districts, plus stints as VP of several private engineering consulting companies.

Gary's also been a Marketing Coordinator and earlier in his career was very likely guilty of at least some of the sins of omission and commission presented in this book. Oops. Sorry about that.

In addition to lessons learned from the School of Hard Knocks, serving on selection committees completely changed how he approaches proposals and presentations.

CLOSING THOUGHT

From the Monty Python film *Life of Brian*

BRIAN
You're all individuals.

THE CROWD
Yes, we're all individuals!

BRIAN
You're all different.

THE CROWD
Yes, we're all different!

ONE LONE VOICE
I'm not.

www.ingramcontent.com/pod-product-compliance
Lightning Source LLC
Chambersburg PA
CBHW032329210326
41518CB00041B/1968